ECHOES OF REFLECTION

THE POETRY COLLECTION OF LAURIE WEISSGARBER

LAURIE JEAN WEISSGARBER

Edited by
LEO VOGEL

Copyright © 2025 by Leo Vogel

All rights reserved.

No part of this book may be reproduced in any form or by any electronic or mechanical means, including information storage and retrieval systems, without written permission from the editor, except for the use of brief quotations in a book review.

Please submit errors to errata@leovogel.com

Print edition set in EB Garamond.

Dedicated to my mom, Laurie.

Laurie Jean Weissgarber

Nov 13, 1963 - May 15, 2023

CONTENTS

Foreword   xix
Leo Vogel

Preface   xxi
Leo Vogel

INTRODUCTION

1. HAVING TO WRITE   3
   Possibly By Laurie Weissgarber

2. POETRY   4
   Possibly By Laurie Weissgarber

FEELINGS

3. COURAGE   7
   Possibly by Laurie Weissgarber

4. GRATITUDE   8
   Possibly by Laurie Weissgarber

5. A SMILE   9
   Possibly by Laurie Weissgarber

6. SOLITUDE   10
   Unknown Author

7. SIMPLICITY   11
   Unknown Author

8. ANTICIPATION   12
   Unknown Author

9. TRANQUILITY   13
   Unknown Author

10. TRUSTING   14
    Possibly by Laurie Weissgarber

11. WONDER IS...   15
    Possibly by Laurie Weissgarber

12. OUTBURST   16
    Possibly by Laurie Weissgarber

13. WEATHERLY EMOTIONS   17
Possibly by Laurie Weissgarber

14. A THOUGHT APART   19
Possibly by Laurie Weissgarber

SCHOOL

15. TEENAGERS   23
Possibly by Laurie Weissgarber

16. PARENT'S ADVICE   25
Possibly by Laurie Weissgarber

17. TALKING ON THE PHONE   26
Possibly by Laurie Weissgarber

18. EYE CONTACT   27
Unknown Author

19. A FANTASY   28
Possibly by Laurie Weissgarber

20. REFLECTIONS (1)   29
Laurie Weissgarber

21. GRADUATION   30
Unknown Author

22. FUTURE   31
Unknown Author

FRIENDSHIP

23. A SPECIAL FRIENDSHIP   35
by Laurie Weissgarber

24. YOU'RE ONE OF MY FAVORITE PEOPLE   36
Possibly By Laurie Weissgarber

25. FRIENDSHIP (1)   37
Possibly By Laurie Weissgarber

26. THREE WISHES   39
Possibly by Laurie Weissgarber

27. BROKEN FRIENDS   40
Possibly by Laurie Weissgarber

28. COME BACK   41
Possibly by Laurie Weissgarber

29. MY BEST FRIEND   42
    Possibly by Laurie Weissgarber

30. YOU HAVE SUCH A POSITIVE OUTLOOK
    ON LIFE   44
    Possibly by Laurie Weissgarber

31. FRIENDS ARE KEEPSAKES   45
    Possibly by Laurie Weissgarber

32. FRIENDSHIP (2)   46
    By Ludwig Van Beethoven

33. SAYINGS   47
    Unknown Author

34. AN AUNT, A FRIEND   48
    Unknown Author

35. THE RIDDLE   49
    Unknown Author

36. IT TAKES MORE THAN WORDS   50
    Unknown Author

37. THE STRONGEST KIND OF LOVE   51
    Unknown Author

38. THINGS UNTOLD, STILL KNOWN   52
    Unknown Author

39. FRIENDSHIP (3)   53
    Unknown Author

40. LET ME BE YOUR FRIEND   54
    Unknown Author

41. FRIENDSHIP POEM   56
    Unknown Author

42. FRIEND   57
    Possibly by Laurie Weissgarber

43. CHANGING   58
    Possibly by Laurie Weissgarber

44. THE JOY OF YOUR FRIENDSHIP   59
    Unknown Author

45. THE MOST PRECIOUS GIFT   60
    Unknown Author

46. FRIENDS ARE RARE Unknown Author	61
47. THE MAGIC OF A FRIEND Unknown Author	62
48. WE MADE EACH OTHER STRONG Unknown Author	63
49. FRIENDSHIP (4) Unknown Author	65
50. I HAVEN'T SEEN YOU IN AWHILE Susan Polis Schutz	66
51. MY FRIEND Possibly by Laurie Weissgarber	67

MEMORIES

52. GATHERING MEMORIES Possibly by Laurie Weissgarber	71
53. MEMORIES (1) Possibly by Laurie Weissgarber	72
54. FOND MEMORIES Possibly by Laurie Weissgarber	73
55. HOLDING ON, LETTING GO Unknown Author	74
56. MEMORIES (2) Unknown Author	75
57. FOR YOU Unknown Author	76

LIFE

58. THE SEA OF LIFE Possibly by Laurie Weissgarber	79
59. LIFE (1) Unknown Author	80
60. STAGE Possibly by Laurie Weissgarber	81
61. LIFE (2) Unknown Author	82

62. IMAGES Unknown Author	83
63. LIFE (3) Unknown Author	84
64. TAKE TIME Unknown Author	85

THE RELATIONSHIP

65. I'M LOOKING AROUND Possibly by Laurie Weissgarber	89
66. WHY GOOD LOOKS by Laurie Weissgarber	90
67. UNTITLED Likely By Laurie Weissgarber	91
68. YOU'RE SPECIAL by Laurie Weissgarber	93
69. TOO GOOD TO BE TRUE by Laurie Weissgarber	94
70. ONLY TIME WILL TELL Possibly by Laurie Weissgarber	95
71. A BEGINNING Possibly by Laurie Weissgarber	96
72. I CAN'T FIGHT THIS FEELING by Laurie Weissgarber	97
73. SONGS REMIND ME OF YOU by Laurie Weissgarber	98
74. MY LOVED ONE Possibly by Laurie Weissgarber	99
75. SUMMER DREAMS (1) Possibly by Laurie Weissgarber	100
76. YOUR PICTURE Possibly by Laurie Weissgarber	101
77. YOU'RE MYSTERIOUS by Laurie Weissgarber	102
78. I NEED TO KNOW Possibly by Laurie Weissgarber	103

79. DIZZY IN LOVE 104
   Possibly by Laurie Weissgarber

80. THINKING OF YOU (1) 105
   Possibly by Laurie Weissgarber

81. SILENCE 106
   Possibly by Laurie Weissgarber

82. IN TOUCH 107
   Possibly by Laurie Weissgarber

83. SATURDAY NIGHT 108
   Possibly by Laurie Weissgarber

84. CINQUAIN 109
   Possibly by Laurie Weissgarber

85. LOVE GAMES 110
   Possibly by Laurie Weissgarber

86. SOMETIMES 111
   Possibly by Laurie Weissgarber

87. LETTING GO 113
   Possibly by Laurie Weissgarber

88. TEARS 114
   Possibly by Laurie Weissgarber

89. FADED 115
   Possibly by Laurie Weissgarber

LOVE

90. LOVE IS.... 119
   Possibly by Laurie Weissgarber

91. LOVE (1) 120
   Possibly by Laurie Weissgarber

92. LOVE (2) 121
   Unknown Author

93. LOVE (3) 123
   Unknown Author

94. I ASK MYSELF 124
   Unknown Author

95. THINKING OF YOU (2) 125
   Unknown Author

96. MAKE IT UP Unknown Author	126
97. YOU Unknown Author	127
98. NEVER BLIND Possibly by Laurie Weissgarber	128
99. COLORFUL GOOD-BYES Unknown Author	129
100. LOVE (4) Possibly by Laurie Weissgarber	130
101. A WISH COME TRUE Unknown Author	131
102. WHAT ARE THESE FEELINGS Unknown Author	132
103. SPECIAL FEELINGS Possibly by Laurie Weissgarber	133
104. TOGETHER Unknown Author	134
105. ONCE IN A LIFETIME Unknown Author	135
106. FORGET ME NOT Unknown Author	136
107. A FRIEND IS AMIE Unknown Author	138
108. LIVING IN THE PAST Unknown Author	140
109. MR. TRUE LOVE Possibly by Laurie Weissgarber	141
110. SHINING Unknown Author	142
111. LET LOVE GROW Unknown Author	143
112. THE PERFECT LOVE Unknown Author	144
113. LOVE (5) Unknown Author	145

114. LOVE (6) Unknown Author	146
115. TRUE LOVE Unknown Author	147
116. LOVE (7) Unknown Author	148
117. THE MYSTERY OF LOVE Unknown Author	149
118. FAR AWAY THOUGHTS Unknown Author	150
119. NOT TO TOUCH Unknown Author	152
120. NEXT TIME Unknown Author	153
121. HIDDEN LOVE Unknown Author	154
122. YOU ONLY HAVE TO SAY "HELLO" Possibly by Laurie Weissgarber	155
123. VALENTINE'S DAY Possibly by Laurie Weissgarber	156
124. YOUR LOVE Possibly by Laurie Weissgarber	157

DREAMS

125. ESCAPE Possibly by Laurie Weissgarber	161
126. REALITY Carrie J. Myers	162
127. SOMETIME... Unknown Author	163
128. ALL YOU CAN BE Unknown Author	164
129. IMAGINATION Unknown Author	165
130. TAKE A CHANCE Unknown Author	166

131. DREAMS Unknown Author	167
132. DREAM YOUR LIFE AWAY Possibly by Laurie Weissgarber	168
133. ALL THAT'S WISHED FOR YOU Possibly by Laurie Weissgarber	169
134. HOLD ON TO YOUR DREAMS Unknown Author	170
135. TO HAVE A DREAM Unknown Author	171

ART

136. WHAT MUSIC CAN DO Possibly by Laurie Weissgarber	175
137. THROUGH AN ARTIST'S EYES Unknown Author	176
138. ARTIST ANONYMOUS Possibly by Laurie Weissgarber	177

OCEAN

139. THE SEA (1) by Laurie Weissgarber	181
140. AN OCEAN OF FEELINGS Possibly by Laurie Weissgarber	182
141. REFLECTIONS (2) Possibly by Laurie Weissgarber	183
142. SEA SHELL Possibly by Laurie Weissgarber	184
143. THE BEACH Possibly by Laurie Weissgarber	185
144. MYSTERIOUS SURFER Possibly by Laurie Weissgarber	186
145. THE SEA (2) Possibly by Laurie Weissgarber	187
146. THE OCEAN (1) Unknown Author	188

147. SEASIDE MOMENTS   189
     Unknown Author

148. THE OCEAN (2)   190
     Unknown Author

149. THE SEA (3)   191
     Unknown Author

150. MEETING AT NIGHT   192
     Robert Browning

151. THE OCEAN (3)   193
     Possibly by Laurie Weissgarber

152. OCEAN ROMANCE   195
     Unknown Author

NATURE

153. THE SANDS OF TIME   199
     Unknown Author

154. CLOUDS   200
     Possibly by Laurie Weissgarber

155. FREE FLIGHT   201
     Possibly by Laurie Weissgarber

156. THINKING OF YOU (3)   203
     Possibly by Laurie Weissgarber

157. SUNSET   204
     Unknown Author

158. DON'T RUSH IN   205
     Possibly by Laurie Weissgarber

159. I'D LIKE TO BE A BIRD   206
     Unknown Author

160. BEFORE THE DOWNPOUR   207
     Unknown Author

161. THE KITE   208
     Possibly by Laurie Weissgarber

162. THE STARS   209
     Possibly by Laurie Weissgarber

163. SHOOTING STARS   210
     Possibly by Laurie Weissgarber

164. GRACE   211
    Unknown Author

165. SANCTUARY   212
    Unknown Author

166. LIVING TREASURES   213
    Unknown Author

167. THE OLD OAK TREE   214
    Possibly by Laurie Weissgarber

168. HARMONY   215
    Unknown Author

169. SINCE THE SUNRISE   216
    Possibly by Laurie Weissgarber

170. SMALL WONDER   217
    Possibly by Laurie Weissgarber

SEASONS

171. SPRING BREEZES   221
    Possibly by Laurie Weissgarber

172. SPRING IS NEAR   222
    Carrie J. Myers

173. CELEBRATION   223
    Unknown Author

174. BEAUTIFUL THINGS   224
    Unknown Author

175. SUMMER VISIONS   225
    Possibly by Laurie Weissgarber

176. SUMMER DREAMS (2)   226
    Unknown Author

177. SUMMER'S END   227
    Unknown Author

178. I AM AUTUMN   228
    Unknown Author

179. FINDING NATURE   229
    Unknown Author

180. GOLDEN Unknown Author	230
181. WINTER Unknown Author	231

OTHER

182. AGE Possibly by Laurie Weissgarber	235
183. GOOD OL' SNOOPY Possibly by Laurie Weissgarber	236
184. MODERN WORLD Possibly by Laurie Weissgarber	237
185. THE LITTLE MERMAID Possibly by Laurie Weissgarber	238
186. TIME Unknown Author	239
187. ENCHANTMENT Unknown Author	240
188. MIRACLES Unknown Author	241
189. I WANT Unknown Author	242
190. YOU ARE SPECIAL Unknown Author	243
191. MOMENTS Unknown Author	244
192. FREE SPIRIT Unknown Author	245
193. WRITING Unknown Author	246
194. REMEMBER ME By Abigail Adams	248

Original Poem Order	249
Photos of Laurie	257
Thanks	273
About the Editor	275
About the Author	277

FOREWORD

LEO VOGEL

Born Laurie Jean Weissgarber, my mother grew up in the beautiful Mid-Hudson Valley and graduated from Dutchess Community College. Laurie was a loving mother of two sons, me and my brother, Ryan. For most of my life, I knew her as Laurie Vogel. In 2015 I attended her second marriage to Steve Harden, a man of unending devotion and love who I will always be grateful to for giving her so much joy and care in her final years with us.

I never knew my mom wrote poetry until after her diagnosis of aphasia. I only discovered her poetry books amongst her arts-and-crafts supplies when she was in the last stage of illness. Some of the poems were discovered on scraps of paper amongst her scrapbooks and college notebooks. It's a bittersweet discovery, as I wish I could have talked to her about her poetry collection and learned more about which poems she had written.

In this book, you will find poems about love, nature, dreams, and friendship. Some of my personal favorites are "Once In a Lifetime", "Three Wishes", and "Hold On To Your Dreams". I consider these poems "lost". Many of the poems with unknown authors are, as far as I know, unpublished in any other book. I have found these poems of unknown authorship quoted in high school yearbooks from across the

United States. I previously didn't know of this poetry collection in the 33 years I knew Laurie before discovering them.

My mom was a creative person, and these poems speak to her lifelong creativity. From what I've learned, she collected these poems throughout her life, starting in high school, and started putting them into her notebooks in 1985, five years before she became a mother. As I read through the original books, I sensed that some of the poems were written to a romantic interest—these poems are collected into a chapter titled "The Relationship".

The poems in this book are a window into the heart a woman full of love, dreams, and kindness. I am grateful for the opportunity to share these poems and her memories with others and bring light to some poems of unknown authorship. I hope that readers will appreciate the beauty of the words within this book as much as I do.

Live. Laugh. Love.

– Leo Vogel (Editor, Laurie Jean's eldest son)

PREFACE

LEO VOGEL

This book contains poems collected into two notebooks by Laurie Jean Harden starting in 1985. The poems were written by various known authors, unknown authors, and by Laurie herself. This edition does not include any poem with a known author under copyright who has not given express written permission to republish.

The book is divided into chapters by topic. Each topic includes an introduction from Laurie taken from her journals and school papers. The introductions give you insight into the author's life and provide context for the poems of that chapter.

Where two poems share the same name such as "Friendship" each poem has been numbered such as "Friendship (1)" and "Friendship (2)" to make it possible to reference each poem in the Original Poem Order list at the end of the book.

Also at the end of the book is a small collection of photos of Laurie throughout her life.

Poems were transcribed to be as accurate to the original as possible to preserve the original author's work as intended.

INTRODUCTION

A little about myself. I am 24 years old 4' 11" in height. Blue eyes and light brown hair. Very quiet and shy! I love M+M's and teddy bears. And also chocolate chip ice cream.

— LAURIE WEISSGARBER

May 1985

1

HAVING TO WRITE

POSSIBLY BY LAURIE WEISSGARBER

It's funny how I have to write
To make my mind feel clear
It makes my thoughts so far away
Seem suddenly so near
It puts a smile on my face
And sets my life at an even pace
It puts my feet back on the floor
And makes me want to write some more.

2

POETRY

POSSIBLY BY LAURIE WEISSGARBER

Poetry is in essence,
Just how we feel and act.
Our thoughts are written down,
Though not always exact.
They have a deeper meaning
Than just what is said
The words come from your heart
And not your head.
For poetry is subtle,
Revealing of the soul,
All of the inner most feelings
That make a person whole.
So as you read poetry,
You've got to take the time,
And catch the meaning hidden
Between the written lines.

FEELINGS

In Junior High, I got to be in Gym Club which allowed me to be the referee for the 7th graders. I got to wear a uniform and got to be absent from certain parts of gym class because I have a heart condition. I was born with a hole in a small part of my heart. Don't worry, I am not going to die of a heart attack! I just won't run marathons. I didn't like that people didn't believe me about my heart condition. I think that I am special because I have a different heartbeat.

— LAURIE WEISSGARBER

Editor's Note
    Laurie had to struggle with her heart condition her whole life. She was right that her heart condition wouldn't be her cause of death. And she was right that she was special; as anyone close to her knew her warmth and kindness; and that she gave the best hugs.

3

COURAGE

POSSIBLY BY LAURIE WEISSGARBER

Whenever my heart is sinking low,
My smile must never let it show.
Whenever the skies are dull and gray,
My laugh must be cheerful anyway,
Whenever I think I'll lose all hope,
I must learn to live and cope
With everyday problems that may arise
That try to hide my smile
Or dim my skies.
For each new day invites me to try,
To find the courage needed to live by.

4

GRATITUDE

POSSIBLY BY LAURIE WEISSGARBER

Thank you
For all you've done,
And for helping me
Through all my trials.
When I was in need,
You were always there
Like you are now.
I thank you
For all you've given me,
And the words
Spoken for my sake.
I cannot express
My gratitudes;
I can only hope
You will once again
Understand,
Thank you

5

A SMILE

POSSIBLY BY LAURIE WEISSGARBER

A smile does wondrous things
Just think of all the joy it brings.
A smile can brighten the darkest room.
When your world seems full of doom,
A smile will make your heart lighter
And the day of those around you seem brighter.
So smile your warmest smile ever
And just see if it doesn't make you feel better!

6

SOLITUDE

UNKNOWN AUTHOR

These are the times I cherish best;
These times of peaceful solitude,
When all the world doth seem at rest
And there is no one to intrude
Upon my world of dreamy bliss,
Of idle thoughts of far away.
What could one ask for save just this,
A quiet spot
At the end of a long day.

7

SIMPLICITY

UNKNOWN AUTHOR

There's a feeling
Of contentment
To be found
In simple things...
A sense of harmony
That calms
Our restless longings
And brings us closer
To the serenity we seek.

8
ANTICIPATION

UNKNOWN AUTHOR

Nurtured by our visions
Of a golden destiny,
Our hopes grow ever stronger...
Reach ever higher...
Seeking
The endless possibilities
Of tomorrow.

9

TRANQUILITY

UNKNOWN AUTHOR

While Queen Anne's lace
Bows with grace
And the willows weep,
The morning glory
Awakens from its sleep.
Among these friends
The peace in my heart
Knows no end.

10

TRUSTING

POSSIBLY BY LAURIE WEISSGARBER

At peace with myself,
I sit alone.
The crystal water,
Although cool, warms my soul.
Not lonely, alone.
Not weak, strong.
Mind open,
Heartfelt.
Never knowing how,
Never feeling why,
Just trusting.

11

WONDER IS...

POSSIBLY BY LAURIE WEISSGARBER

Wonder is the Niagara Falls,
seeing a movie.
Wonder is being with someone you love.
Wonder is having a special friend,
pretty sunsets and stormy skies.
Wonder is friendship,
and what will happen the next day....

12

OUTBURST

POSSIBLY BY LAURIE WEISSGARBER

The storm is supposedly over,
But there in my room,
With my stinging throat
And my outburst lip,
I am still defiant.
The angry thoughts boil over
Like clouds rolling in;
The air is alertly still,
Threating to rain
On my sunny day.
I know the argument is over,
But I can still see the lightning;
It's etched upon my eyelids
When the house is dark -
The ghost of my angry words.

13

WEATHERLY EMOTIONS

POSSIBLY BY LAURIE WEISSGARBER

Rain,
Pouring down from the skies
Like the stream of tears
Running down my face
As I think of when we parted.
Sun,
Shining bright
Making me smile
As I think of the times
Spent with you.
Rainbow,
Beautiful to see
I smile and cry
As I think of the wonderful memories
That you left me.
Weather,
So much like my emotions
Different day to day
Wishing the rain and tears would go

POSSIBLY BY LAURIE WEISSGARBER

Hoping you and the sun
Would forever stay.

14

A THOUGHT APART

POSSIBLY BY LAURIE WEISSGARBER

I should like to rise and go,
To a place where the sun shall forever show.
Where beyond the meadows an ocean lies,
With waters as brilliant as the sunlit skies.
To a land where singing seagulls soar,
As the waves greet the wind
With a crashing roar.
The essence of spring flowers would fill the air,
Lacing the earth in floral fair.
And if the sky may darken
Or if the snow may fall,
I could think none of it and turn away from
    it all.
I'll escape to my paradise
Beyond this land so cold in heart,
And wonder through my dreamland
Just a thought apart.

SCHOOL

In high school I had to study more and harder than my sister or brother but I got through. Classes I enjoyed the most were: Family Life, Children's Literature, Cooking, and Social Studies. Everyone used to think I was the teacher's pet and a goody goody. The first part I didn't care about because someday I knew I wanted to be a teacher; but the second part hurt. I didn't have a big crowd of friends, but the group I had was a lot of fun. We used to wait for each other after class and meet each other at our lockers. We would try to eat lunch together so that we wouldn't have to eat lunch alone!

— LAURIE WEISSGARBER

15

TEENAGERS

POSSIBLY BY LAURIE WEISSGARBER

A teenager's world is not a pleasant place to be,
In a teenagers eye's you can see anger,
The hatred for the world that's trying to change them.
And for the so-called adults who tell them to grow up.
But teenagers don't want to grow up.
They see no reason to
Their world may be mixed up, but they like it,
It's full of kids trying to find themselves,
Trying to fit in
When you're a teenager, you're out to see what you like,
You're out to do what you want to do,
Not what others want you to do or become.
Everyone was a teenager once,
But no one seems to remember.
No one remembers the angry, lonely, frustrating,

POSSIBLY BY LAURIE WEISSGARBER

Mixed-up life of teenagers,
Or maybe no one wants to!

16

PARENT'S ADVICE

POSSIBLY BY LAURIE WEISSGARBER

As we grow up, we sit and listen to
our parents advice
Of similar situations they had
once or twice.
They don't want us to make
the same mistakes they did,
Acting on impulse —
not using their head.
So cut them some slack,
just kick back and listen
to what they say.
'Cause I'm sure there are times
when they wish
they would have listened.
When they sat where we sit today.

17

TALKING ON THE PHONE

POSSIBLY BY LAURIE WEISSGARBER

My favorite past time is talking on the phone,
It's what I like to do when I'm alone.
I can talk for hours about nothing at all
To practically anyone who happens to call.
To find out the latest on who's dating who,
And talk about problems and gossip too,
Comparing homework and talk about
The latest fads and which clothes are out.
While deciding on which outfit to wear the
    next day,
My mom yells up the steps and I hear her say,
"Get off the phone, you've been on long
    enough,
I'm sure you've gossiped about enough stuff,
Concluding my chat, I return with a sigh;
My friend says, "See ya tomorrow" –
And I say "goodbye!"

18

EYE CONTACT

UNKNOWN AUTHOR

I see you in the hall –
A distant speck that my eyes are trained to
    recognize.
You draw closer –
My heart quickens as I seek
Those familiar eyes.
Your eyes meet mine
And I long for a sign
That you really do see
My heart leaps with joy
As you give me that look.
Then slowly, ever so slowly,
You smile at me.

19

A FANTASY

POSSIBLY BY LAURIE WEISSGARBER

As you led me onto the dance floor
Holding my hand,
I saw him look at me,
The guy in the band.
You held me close –
He smiled at me,
I fell in love
With a fantasy.

20

REFLECTIONS (1)

LAURIE WEISSGARBER

I remember when I was just starting high school
I was nervous and excited
Now as I look to graduation,
It seems that the year just flew by.
I remember all the studying and homework
    assignments.
All the rain days and sunny days,
But as I relive my high school
Years as a senior it is the best!
Being able to write anything you want
Under your picture in the yearbook,
And going to Great Adventure.
Listening to the sounds of the lockers and bells.
And college here I come....

21

GRADUATION

UNKNOWN AUTHOR

Graduation is a time for many emotions.
It is a time for caps and gowns,
A time to celebrate,
A time for high school to end and college to begin.
It is a time to say goodbye to good friends.

22

FUTURE

UNKNOWN AUTHOR

At times I get to thinking
Of where I want to go,
What I want to accomplish—
It's something I must know.
I have to look ahead and see
Just what is in store for me.
The future may be unclear,
But it's something I do not fear.

FRIENDSHIP

    I would like to tell you about a very special person named Mary. She has been [one of] my best friend[s] for [over] 10 years. I met Mary in 4th grade at Overlook Elementary School. We were friends for a year and I lived right around the corner from her, then I moved away.

    We tell each other our deepest secrets and really care about each other. We give each other advice and support. We have gone through good times and bad but that's what friendship is all about. Mary and I have been in [my sister's] wedding, went to concerts, plays, amusement parks, and to Boston together.

    We had fun in high school and when we got older we had fun going to the movies and discos.

    Mary is warm, kind, sincere, truthful, honest, outgoing, fun to be with, helpful, supportive, [a] party animal, a very good listener, and [a] great friend.

— LAURIE WEISSGARBER

23

A SPECIAL FRIENDSHIP

BY LAURIE WEISSGARBER

You and I have a special friendship
that has become stronger.
Our special friendship is based on
honesty and trust.
We show affection and care.
We are there for each other in
good times and bad times.
We don't have to feel threatened
by other people because other people
won't replace the friendship we share!
What is nice is that we share our
little secrets with each other that
we won't tell anyone else.
When we have something on our minds
that is bothering one of us, or both of us,
we can talk about it.
I know we don't see each other often,
but when we do it's special!!!
We can be ourselves to laugh,
talk, and just spend time together.

24

YOU'RE ONE OF MY FAVORITE PEOPLE

POSSIBLY BY LAURIE WEISSGARBER

Of all the people I have known
It seems so few possess
A sense of genuine concern
For someone's happiness...
So that's why I consider you
A friend among all friends
Who has the human qualities
That life so rarely sends...
And I can't think of anything
More wonderful or fine
Than just to know you'll always be
A favorite friend of mine...

25

FRIENDSHIP (1)

POSSIBLY BY LAURIE WEISSGARBER

In the years before we met
The friends I had were few,
I always wished that I would
Get a friend as dear as you.
I remember that stormy argument
And I was on your side,
I understood your problems,
And in you I could confide.
I had a beautiful thought
So far up in my mind,
That you were the one to be my friend
Because you were so kind.
I knew I had to find a way
To show you that I cared,
So I thanked you on that special day
For the friendship that we shared.
I was glad that you were here
To help pass the time of day,
And I never had a fear
That you would go away.

POSSIBLY BY LAURIE WEISSGARBER

I remembered that one late last night.
When you tried to make me see,
That everything would be all right
Between both you and me.
Then the day was finally here
For you to say good-bye,
And I became so full of fear
But I tried hard not to cry.
The next few days were the worst,
Because all I did was try,
To tell myself it would be okay,
But all I did was cry.
Now I look upon the days
Of the friendship that we shared,
And everything you said to me
Showed me that you cared.
And you still care so much
That the amount will never end.
Because we both care for each other so much
And it makes me very proud to be your best
    friend, and sister.

26

THREE WISHES

POSSIBLY BY LAURIE WEISSGARBER

If I could have three wishes
I'd be hoping, first of all
That maybe you'd surprise me
With an unexpected call...
And then, I'd wish that somehow
We could have a friendly chat
With both of us exchanging
Little bits of this and that...
And third — but most important
I'd be hoping that we two
Could get to see each other
Much more often than we do...

27

BROKEN FRIENDS

POSSIBLY BY LAURIE WEISSGARBER

Wasn't it yesterday that we were friends?
Wasn't it yesterday that we were making
    amends?
Scheming and ruling, we had it all down,
Loving and living the niche we had found.
Friends we were, "together til the end!"
And when in trouble, a helping hand we would
    lend.
But that was yesterday, now it's today.
Broken promises erupted, I guess we all pay.
When the trust is forgotten, so it the friend.
Now the best we can offer is to start over again.

28

COME BACK

POSSIBLY BY LAURIE WEISSGARBER

So many things
Remind me of you.
Things we used to talk about,
Things we used to do.
All the times we spent
Making future plans.
Believing everything you said to me,
My heart was in your hands.
Everything is different now,
A part of you has changed.
I can't seem to understand it,
My life's all rearranged.
I hope someday that we'll go back
To the way it used to be.
I miss you more than you could know,
So please come back to me.

29

MY BEST FRIEND

POSSIBLY BY LAURIE WEISSGARBER

My life was a disaster
Nothing I could think of was good
Until I talked to you
You cheered me up the best you could.
I laughed at what I once cried
Because of you
I look at the world differently now,
I am no longer blue.
You stood by me
When I didn't even want to hang on
I gave you ever reason to leave me,
Without you I would be gone.
There is no way I can repay you
Even when the whole world was against me
I could turn around and see you
Smiling, and instead of saying me you said we.
I am so lucky to have you here
No one else could possibly have a best friend
    like you.

My Best Friend

With you I have nothing to fear
I just wanted to say thanks for being so dear!

30

YOU HAVE SUCH A POSITIVE OUTLOOK ON LIFE

POSSIBLY BY LAURIE WEISSGARBER

You have such a
Positive outlook on life
Your words are always encouraging
Your face is lit up with excitement
Your actions are so straight forward
Your inner strength helps you to
Achieve so much
When people are around you
They seem to absorb your uplifting attitude
When I think about you
I can only think
Of how lucky I am
To know you.

31

FRIENDS ARE KEEPSAKES

POSSIBLY BY LAURIE WEISSGARBER

Friends are keepsakes
So precious and rare –
Keepsakes to cherish
And handle with care…
Friends are treasures
Much richer than gold –
Treasures intended
To have and to hold…
They're timeless blessings,
The greatest by far
Especially when someone's
The friend that you are…

32

FRIENDSHIP (2)

BY LUDWIG VAN BEETHOVEN

Never shall I forget
the days which I spent with you.
Continue to be my friend,
As you will always find me yours.

33

SAYINGS

UNKNOWN AUTHOR

He who finds a friend finds a treasure
And from that moment on
He knows no matter where he walks
His lonely days are gone
Though we travel the world
Over to find the beautiful,
We must carry it with us
Or we will find it not.
It is a chance that
Makes brothers
But hearts
That make friends.

34

AN AUNT, A FRIEND

UNKNOWN AUTHOR

Rainbows are made with magic,
Hopes and dreams.
They fill the air with serenity,
So powerful they seem.
Their colors shine with attraction,
Glow and gleam.
Reaching out to others,
Happiness they bring.
I know someone special,
Full of colors so bright.
She could be a rainbow
If it were her right.
A friend, she is always there
With understanding and love.
To everyone she is special,
Especially to the family she is a part of.

35

THE RIDDLE

UNKNOWN AUTHOR

Who am I?
I am deeper than the deepest ocean
I am covert, yet free
I am built upon love and anchored by trust —
I am Friendship.

36

IT TAKES MORE THAN WORDS
UNKNOWN AUTHOR

It takes more than words
To let you know
How much it means to me
To have you as a friend.
I can depend on you for understanding,
When I am confused.
I can depend on you for comfort,
When I am sad.
I can depend on you for laughter,
When I am happy,
I am so thankful
To know that you are
Always
My friend.

37

THE STRONGEST KIND OF LOVE
UNKNOWN AUTHOR

Smiles come easier;
Laughter sounds sweeter
In unison.
Fears and troubles grow quiet
When listened to
With understanding.
Two who walk a road together
Walk farther than someone alone.
Friendship is the strongest kind of love.

38

THINGS UNTOLD, STILL KNOWN

UNKNOWN AUTHOR

Our friendship is as deep as any sea,
We know each other so thoroughly.
Your eyes are like windows
Through which I can see the emotions flow.
Every thought, triumph, disappointment is visible.
Behind your eyes, there for me to see.
Even though your face says happy,
I can see the sadness hidden behind your eyes.
In a way it's kind of funny,
For you and I are as different as can be.
Though different as we are,
Somehow we belong together,
Like stars in the heavens
And sand on the shore.
Our friendship will always be,
Forever and ever – eternally.
We know this though it's never been said,
For it's a thing untold, but still known.

39

FRIENDSHIP (3)

UNKNOWN AUTHOR

Friendship defies age
And ignores distance.
It weathers the hard times
And shares the good;
Together we have found this.
Our friendship has provided acceptance
And understanding in a world
That pushes people apart.
But I will always remain
With the memories
Of the times we have shared
Knowing how fortunate I am
To be able to call you my friend.

40

LET ME BE YOUR FRIEND

UNKNOWN AUTHOR

I'd like to capture a rainbow
And stick it in a big box
So that,
Anytime you wanted to,
You can reach in and pull out
A piece of sunshine.
I'd like to build you a mountain
That you could call your very own
A place to find serenity
In those times when you feel the need to be
Closer to yourself....
I'd like to be the one
Who's there with you when you're
Lonely or troubled
Or you just need
Someone
To hold on to.
I'd like to do all this and more
To make your life happy.
But, sometimes

Let Me Be Your Friend

It isn't easy to do
The things I would like to do
Or give the things I would like to give.
So...until I learn how to catch rainbows and
    build mountains,
Let me do for you that which I know best...
...Let me simply
Be your friend.

41

FRIENDSHIP POEM

UNKNOWN AUTHOR

You're that special kind of friend
That everyone wishes they could have.
I always know when we're apart
That we're still so close,
And when we're together
Our time will be spent
Enjoying it to the fullest.
It's not everyone that can
have a special friend like you.
I'm proud to say that I do.

42

FRIEND

POSSIBLY BY LAURIE WEISSGARBER

If you ever need a friend,
I have a lot of love to share.
I will be here until the end,
To show how much I really care.
If you ever need a guide
To help you see the light,
I will be right by your side
To make everything seem bright.
If you're ever looking for love,
You have to look no more.
For I will show you a side of love
That you have never seen before.
So, if you're ever feeling blue,
Just remember I love you.

43

CHANGING

POSSIBLY BY LAURIE WEISSGARBER

Hey, here's looking at you
And what you want to be
And what you want to do.
But I need some time
To grow and live
And give you all
I want to give.
If you don't see things my way
That's all right, I understand.
But please don't turn away
When I hold out my hand,
Because you're my friend
I have nothing to hide.
If you want, I'll still be there
When you're hurting inside.
So, friend, remember –
Changing isn't a crime.
It's a wonderful experience
That happens with time.

44

THE JOY OF YOUR FRIENDSHIP

UNKNOWN AUTHOR

This morning in the early light
I thought of you a while
And as I blinked my sleepy eyes
My heart began to smile...
For I recalled your friendliness,
Your own good-natured ways,
The laughter and the memories
Of happy yesterdays...
Then as I rose to the meet the day
I felt so warm inside
To know your friendship's given me
A sense of joy and pride...

45

THE MOST PRECIOUS GIFT

UNKNOWN AUTHOR

Life is filled with many gifts
Beyond our fondest dreams —
The shady trees, the meadow lands,
The silver lakes and streams...
The morning sun, the evening stars,
The blue sky high above,
The breezes of a summer day,
The cooing of a dove...
But in my mind, the greatest one
That there could ever be
Is friendship — the most precious gift
That you have given me...

46

FRIENDS ARE RARE

UNKNOWN AUTHOR

Acquaintances may come and go
But friends are rare indeed
Because in every phase of life
They fill a special need...
And since you're just that kind of friend
On whom I can rely
I find myself at ease with you
Whenever you're nearby...
So whether we are face to face
Or whether we're apart
You hold a most important place
Within my grateful heart...

47

THE MAGIC OF A FRIEND
UNKNOWN AUTHOR

It's the little things that matter,
The unexpected things.
The thoughtful gift that gives a lift,
The thrill phone call brings!
The kindly deed for one in need,
The willingness to share.
The happy smile that helps awhile
And tells someone, "I care!"

48

WE MADE EACH OTHER STRONG
UNKNOWN AUTHOR

My friend, I do not wish for you to go,
But life will not wait for us, I know.
Don't look back and see the tears
Streaking down my face.
In my heart you'll never be replaced.
Hold tight to today and it will take you to
    tomorrow
Hold your head high and you will see that the
    sorrow
Will soon fade with a dream that is yet to be.
We're going to be.
We're going to be the best of all, just you wait
    and see!
Take me with you when you go,
I'll stay forever in your heart.
That way we'll never have to say we lost a part of
    ourselves.
You're just the part of me I can't let go,
And I thank God you are a friend I'll always
    know.

UNKNOWN AUTHOR

So thank you for growing up with me, my friend.
Parting now, we'll reach for the stars, and see it's not an end,
But the beginning of a life we've dreamt of for so long.
Wow its time to show the world – we've made each other strong!

49

FRIENDSHIP (4)

UNKNOWN AUTHOR

I thank you for all the times you cared
And all the moments that we shared
I thank you for the memories
A friend to me you'll always be.
I thank you for your tenderness
That fills each day with happiness
A joy that lasts eternally
A friend to me you'll always be.
I thank you for being there
And all the things you had to bear
And though there are times we don't agree
A friend to me you'll always be.
I thank you for the gift of love
A gift that's sent from Heaven above
A love that is purity
A friend to me you'll always be.
I thank you for the things I see
And what our friendship shows to me
I'll thank you for eternity
A friend to me you'll always be.

50

I HAVEN'T SEEN YOU IN AWHILE

SUSAN POLIS SCHUTZ

I haven't seen you in awhile
yet I often imagine
all your expressions

I haven't spoken to you recently
but many times
I hear your thoughts

Good friends must not always
    be together
It is the feeling of oneness
    when distant
that proves a lasting friendship

— SUSAN POLIS SCHUTZ

The poem "I haven't seen you in awhile" by Susan Polis Schutz is used by permission. Copyright © 1976 by Continental Publications. Renewed copyright © 2022 by Stephen Schutz and Susan Polis Schutz. All rights reserved.

51

MY FRIEND

POSSIBLY BY LAURIE WEISSGARBER

She will always help when in need,
Handing out advice as you plead.
Ever need a friend?
Right there she will be,
Ready to listen and to see
You through your sorrows, till the end.

MEMORIES

My teachers advised me to continue my education past high school. I was trying to figure out if I could get financial aid for college. I also had to think if I could handle all the work and many hours of studying for each class. It was hard for me to decide which career I was interested in.

I knew I was interested in working with children. I have enjoyed helping my younger cousins with their homework. I didn't want to sit at a desk or work with computers. So I decided to become a Nursery School teacher.

I am looking forward to getting my A.A.S. Degree in Early Childhood.

— LAURIE WEISSGARBER

Editor's Note

Laurie didn't work as a nursery school teacher but she did work in childcare services throughout her career including owning a daycare for a period in the 1990's.

52

GATHERING MEMORIES

POSSIBLY BY LAURIE WEISSGARBER

Often times when I'm in need
Of just a little smile
I search a memory or two
And think of you awhile...
And you would really be surprised
How thoughts of you create
The nicest feelings in my heart
That I appreciate...
So you can see how much it means
To leave my cares behind
By gathering these memories
That keep you on my mind...

53

MEMORIES (1)

POSSIBLY BY LAURIE WEISSGARBER

Memories tucked away
Upstairs in an old chest
Of the times we had spent.
Pictures and old love letters
Made the tears fall.
What happened?
Was it me?
We had so much fun –
Holding hands, days we spent
In the sun.
Now its gone.
As I shut the chest
The memories are once again
Tucked away,
But not forgotten.

54

FOND MEMORIES

POSSIBLY BY LAURIE WEISSGARBER

Looking over my shoulder
Through the mist on the path of the past
I see times that we shared together
Times where no dim shadows were cast.
Holding each other's hand
We would walk for what seemed like miles.
Telling each other our secrets
Watching each other smile.
Those times ended so very long ago
And now we've grown apart
But I'll never forget our special moments.
The memories linger on in my heart.

55

HOLDING ON, LETTING GO

UNKNOWN AUTHOR

The new year comes,
And the old year's past,
It seemed to me to go too fast.
If only I could hold onto it,
Forever and ever
Reliving it and letting go of it never.
Thinking of the days
Of this wonderful year
Trying to remember without a tear.
Well, I can't make it stay
With anything I might say,
But the memories will
Carry on with me.

56

MEMORIES (2)

UNKNOWN AUTHOR

Memories
Always brighten up my day
When things are going wrong.
Memories
Are what I think of
Whenever they play our song.
Memories
Are there to look back on,
To remember times we shared.
Memories
Are what I'm trapped in,
Because I know you're no longer there.

57

FOR YOU

UNKNOWN AUTHOR

Once,
I loved you
Sometimes
I miss you
Always
I'll care for you.
Never
Will I forget you.

LIFE

*If you want to improve your life,
go out and play a game of tennis.*

— LAURIE WEISSGARBER

58

THE SEA OF LIFE

POSSIBLY BY LAURIE WEISSGARBER

My heart pounds
    as I gasp for breath.
My world crashes
    like the waves of an untamed sea.
One moment I'm riding high,
    looking down upon the world.
Then the wave crashes
    and more roll in.
Confusing and tumbling,
I'm lost in the chaos,
Wondering each time
    if I'll come out on top,
Or if the waves of confusion
    will conquer
And I will be lost in the sea.

59

LIFE (1)

UNKNOWN AUTHOR

Life can travel in circles
When your destiny remains unknown
People and places behind you
Mean nothing when you're alone.
You can be the master
Of your destiny
Leave yesterday's footprints behind you
And choose where today's lead.
Follow a rainbow, reach for a star,
Put them in your pocket and you'll go far.
Never let your dreams die,
Don't tell yourself a lie.
You can make it, don't you fake it,
Try!

60

STAGE

POSSIBLY BY LAURIE WEISSGARBER

Sometimes I wonder about God's great stage.
We play the roles so well.
But who are we playing for,
And when will it end?
We do the same scenes over and over again,
And we still make the same mistakes.
We never learn.
We play our roles no matter who it hurts,
Not even if it's us.

61

LIFE (2)

UNKNOWN AUTHOR

Life, at times, seems so unfair.
But all we can do is learn and share.
The ladder of life is the toughest to climb
And growing up should be the first step in mind.
Making choices is what we all go through.
Living by the choice is sometimes hard to do.
Taking chances is scary at first,
Especially when it's you who may get hurt.
Getting hurt isn't something any of us want,
But it makes us stronger-stronger in the heart.
We can only learn from the mistakes we make
And hope that the next time it's the right road that we take.

62

IMAGES

UNKNOWN AUTHOR

Waiting in unseen depths...
Bursting forth
In myriads of images
And patterns...
Life is ever renewing itself...
Flowing endlessly
Through all creation.

63

LIFE (3)

UNKNOWN AUTHOR

Time
Life's most precious gift.
Love
Life's best feeling.
Friendship
Life's most valuable possession.
Without time
All is lost.
Without love
Who cares.
Without friendship
Nothing matters.
Time, Love, Friendship —
The elements of life.

64

TAKE TIME

UNKNOWN AUTHOR

Take time to enjoy life.
To laugh and cry.
Take each day as it comes,
But don't let life pass you by.
Take time to recall the good times
Shared with old friends and loves
But don't live in the past.

Take time to wonder
What the future may bring,
But live for today,
Because today is everything.
Take time to share yourself
With friends and family too
And remember to
Take time to love
Because only those who love
Can be loved too.

THE RELATIONSHIP

On my first day [at Dutchess Community College] I was excited to meet new people, but I was also a little nervous. It is a big difference not being in high school anymore. It gives you a chance to meet more people and talk about different curriculums. Everyone was running around trying to find their classes. People were somewhat unsure if they should talk to strange people they didn't know. In all my classes I was also at the end of the alphabet.

In my first cycling class, I started talking to two girls Barbara and Pam. I also [noticed a guy that I knew, from a party], named Paul.

In cycling class we had a lot of fun. We rode on trips over and around the college. Our class at the beginning was a group of strangers, but as the weeks came and went we had a lot of laughs. We went on trips to coffee shops, the main mall, and the Hudson River Psychiatric Center.

— LAURIE WEISSGARBER

65

I'M LOOKING AROUND

POSSIBLY BY LAURIE WEISSGARBER

Only give me a guy who's not stereotypical,
Who's kind and thoughtful and analytical,
Not anxious to impress or scare another,
His own person, not hiding under the cover
Of looks or muscles, all talk and tricks,
Someone to whom I'd happily stick.
A man among men, an individual of pride,
Instead of those boys I find at my side.
Mother Nature, please help these boys
    become men,
For I'm all grown up and anxious for when
I can meet and talk to and look up to and share
My life and love with someone who cares!

66

WHY GOOD LOOKS

BY LAURIE WEISSGARBER

Why do people care so much
about good looks?
The person's personality
is what really counts.
I should give the person a chance
The person is probably the nicest,
warmest and caring and sensitive
person I could know.
I should stop comparing him
with other guys.
Because he does have beautiful blue eyes.
Maybe it's just that I am confused
And unsure if I like him.
But I would like to get to know him.

67

UNTITLED

LIKELY BY LAURIE WEISSGARBER

Editor's Note: This was written to an unknown person. Laurie made a note to herself to write the person's name in but she never did—the recipient remains a mystery. However, I believe it is a man named Russ G. who was a love interest of Laurie's when she was a student at Dutchess Community College.

I can read your eyes
Like an open book.
I can tell your thoughts
In one quick look.
I just look at your eyes
With their light blue gaze.
You think you can hide them
From me, don't you?
Your expression is one
That is forced, I see.
You're trying to keep
Your feelings from me.
Don't waste your time,
I can still see through

LIKELY BY LAURIE WEISSGARBER

That emotionless stare
To the real, inner you.
It's not at all hard
To read your mind.
But I can also tell
When they're filled with care.
Why it is your eyes say
What your mouth wouldn't dare?

YOU'RE SPECIAL

BY LAURIE WEISSGARBER

You're special in my ways;
You care so much about people's feelings.
Your smile warms my heart.
Your eyes are so beautiful.
Your body is so slim and muscular.
Your hands are soft but strong
enough for me to feel secure when
holding your hand.
I never saw you get mad
But I won't want to.
Your personality is wonderful
And I would never change it;
Because you're special to me.....

69

TOO GOOD TO BE TRUE

BY LAURIE WEISSGARBER

I feel that it is too good to be true.
I could fall in love with you!
It was like a miracle that we met.
You walked into my life,
We shared some crazy times and some really
    wonderful times,
I hope that we can stay close
I don't want it to be just friends,
It would be really nice to say special friends.
But it is not all up to me.
It is also up to you.
We are friends, but I want to say "special
    friends".
But maybe it is too good to be true.

70

ONLY TIME WILL TELL

POSSIBLY BY LAURIE WEISSGARBER

As the setting sun leaves a golden
shimmer upon the peaceful waters
I begin to think of you.
Hair of silky blond and eyes of deep blue.
We share a perfect friendship
to top off high school years,
But sometimes only friends
can bring me to tears.
I get so confused
with all my mixed-up feelings.
Should I hold onto what we have
or risk it all for more?
Sometimes I even wonder what I'm hoping for.
Hopefully, someday everything will work out
    well.
But with you, only time will tell.

71

A BEGINNING

POSSIBLY BY LAURIE WEISSGARBER

I see you sitting there
With tears in your eyes
I don't know what to say, but
I'm sorry if I made you cry.
It's better to let your feelings show
Then try to hold them in.
To trust and understand someone
Is where things must begin.

70

ONLY TIME WILL TELL

POSSIBLY BY LAURIE WEISSGARBER

As the setting sun leaves a golden
shimmer upon the peaceful waters
I begin to think of you.
Hair of silky blond and eyes of deep blue.
We share a perfect friendship
to top off high school years,
But sometimes only friends
can bring me to tears.
I get so confused
with all my mixed-up feelings.
Should I hold onto what we have
or risk it all for more?
Sometimes I even wonder what I'm hoping for.
Hopefully, someday everything will work out
    well.
But with you, only time will tell.

71

A BEGINNING

POSSIBLY BY LAURIE WEISSGARBER

I see you sitting there
With tears in your eyes
I don't know what to say, but
I'm sorry if I made you cry.
It's better to let your feelings show
Then try to hold them in.
To trust and understand someone
Is where things must begin.

72

I CAN'T FIGHT THIS FEELING

BY LAURIE WEISSGARBER

I have tried so hard to fight this feeling,
What started out as friendship;
Has become stronger.
I've tried to think of you as a special friend
But I want you as more.
I know how you feel about just
Keeping our relationship as "friends".
It's just that you blow my mind
With all the nice things you do for me!
You brighten up my day when
I spend time with you.

73

SONGS REMIND ME OF YOU

BY LAURIE WEISSGARBER

I can't fight this feeling any more,
Because I am crazy for you.
I know all I want to do is dance,
But what about romance.
I'm missing you because you brighten up
    my day.
You have a way about you that sometimes is out
    of touch.
I wish I knew what the method of modern
    love was.
Because if I could I would run to you.
Then I would feel like my sweet dreams are
    coming true.
Because being without you is a hard habit to
    break.
Because you are one in a million.
But maybe that was yesterday;
Because some things are better left unsaid.
But I can dream about you!!

74

MY LOVED ONE

POSSIBLY BY LAURIE WEISSGARBER

Loved one, I need you —
Like a baby, his mother,
Like a forest, the trees.
Your embraces keep me warm
Like the sun to the earth.
Your eyes send me a chill
Like the breeze of autumn.
Your being near calms my fear.

75

SUMMER DREAMS (1)

POSSIBLY BY LAURIE WEISSGARBER

I see your silhouette
In the dark of the night
Looking so lonely, and I join you
With the moon for our light.
The calm water seems to dance
When lit by the light of the moon
I treasure each moment here with you
And dread that it will be over soon.
A cluster of thoughts
Run through my mind
I think of you here with me
So loving, so caring, so kind.
I treasure the time we spend together
The days fly by so it seems.
Always hold on to our memories
We'll build our future on summer dreams.

76

YOUR PICTURE
POSSIBLY BY LAURIE WEISSGARBER

When I look into your picture —
The only part I have of you,
I look into your eyes,
Your beautiful blue eyes,
I look to see what you're thinking.
I'm reading your mind.
Who do you love?
Do you love me?
I love you?

77

YOU'RE MYSTERIOUS

BY LAURIE WEISSGARBER

Why won't you let me into your world?
I want to know your feelings and what interests
 you!
Sometimes I feel that you close me out of your
 world.
If something is bothering you, we could talk
 about it.
I can't read your mind!
I don't want to know everything
Because some things are just your thoughts
No one else's.
Why don't you open up to me?
I hope that you trust me.
I won't judge you for your feelings
And thoughts.
If our thoughts and feelings don't
Agree we can talk about them.
Why are you so mysterious?
– Please Tell Me –

78

I NEED TO KNOW

POSSIBLY BY LAURIE WEISSGARBER

I really need to know the truth
Of exactly how you feel,
I want to know if it's just a game,
Or if your love is real.
I wish that I could tell you
That I think our love is right,
But I don't dare, because I fear
You're with someone else tonight.
Who knows? Maybe it could be only
My imagination running wild.
But please, be honest and sincere with me
And don't treat me like a child,
If you say you really care
And look me straight in the eye,
Than I will also care for you
Otherwise...Goodbye.

79

DIZZY IN LOVE

POSSIBLY BY LAURIE WEISSGARBER

Each time I see you my heart skips a beat,
You do something to me,
I can't even eat.
Going around with my head in a cloud
I can't hear, even when the teacher talks loud.
Everyone's asking me why I'm so dizzy,
I smile coyly and say I am busy.
All the characteristics I said above
Will assure you I'm a girl in love.

80

THINKING OF YOU (1)

POSSIBLY BY LAURIE WEISSGARBER

Thoughts of you fill my mind like
waves upon the shore.
Sunny days and star-filled nights
remind me of you more.
Contentment coming from within to
warm the coldest heart.
Security that strengthens bonds,
never to be torn apart.

81

SILENCE

POSSIBLY BY LAURIE WEISSGARBER

Silence
As loud as a drum,
Steadily pounding.
If only you were to speak —
To even murmur
What is on your mind.
Yell!
Scream!
Holler!
Please do something.
Don't just sit there.

82

IN TOUCH

POSSIBLY BY LAURIE WEISSGARBER

As the butterflies glide with the breeze
The birds cheerfully sing in the trees.
We walk together hand in hand
Across this beautiful land.
Your splendid beauty makes me stare,
The sun gleaming through your woven hair,
As you gaze with eyes tender and true
All thoughts in my head are focused on you.
Sitting by a brook that bubbles on,
Our feelings flowing right along.
When I hold you close to me
Our hearts become entangled for eternity.
If you ever slip away
It would be a tragic day.
Alone I'd sit and cry in pain
While memories of you wash away with the rain.

83

SATURDAY NIGHT

POSSIBLY BY LAURIE WEISSGARBER

I'm sitting here alone,
another Saturday night,
I begged you to come over,
but you only said "I might".
I slowly turn on the TV,
Only to see our song playing on mTV.
I can't help but worry,
I wonder where you are.
For all I know you could be
crashed up in a car.
Honey, please be careful,
I think as I turn out the light.
And please, please don't cheat on me
this lonely Saturday night.
Why should I worry?
You don't seem to really care.
I'm sitting alone on Saturday night,
hugging my teddy bear.

84

CINQUAIN

POSSIBLY BY LAURIE WEISSGARBER

Apology
humble, soft
whisper of admittance
anger vanishing into hope
Smile

85

LOVE GAMES

POSSIBLY BY LAURIE WEISSGARBER

You say that you love me
Then leave me again.
Stop playing the love games
Where I never win.
I thought when I met you
Your feelings were true.
You said you loved me,
If only I knew.
So when you get bored
Or desperate or down,
Don't come running to me,
I won't be around.
Because love's not a game
Where the winner is you.
Love's an emotion
Shared between two.

86

SOMETIMES

POSSIBLY BY LAURIE WEISSGARBER

Sometimes it's so hard
when you love someone so much
to let them walk away.
To stand tall and still
and to watch them leave
when the one thing you want most in the
world is to speak up and call them back.
Sometimes, it's so hard
when you need someone, so much
to think of their needs above your own.
To remember that to hold them
down is to obscure their growth.
To admit that things could never really be just
    right,
and to reflect on what could have been
instead of what will be.
Sometimes it's hard
to keep in mind that silence is golden
and that your silence is the key

POSSIBLY BY LAURIE WEISSGARBER

to someone else's happiness, and sometimes, it's so hard to love someone enough to forget them!

87

LETTING GO

POSSIBLY BY LAURIE WEISSGARBER

Return address
Of a distant city.
Plain envelope,
My name printed
In faded ink.
Corners worn
To a rounded edge,
Stationary warped
With tears
Handwriting barely legible,
I strain my eyes to
Read it over
And over.
I grasp the page
And won't let go
For fear I'd be
Letting go of
Him
And my dreams.

88

TEARS

POSSIBLY BY LAURIE WEISSGARBER

A tear is a token of emotion
It slides down your cheek
Reflecting your feelings
In a quiet and releasing way
It falls and shatters into
A million pieces of hurt
Never to be felt again.

89

FADED

POSSIBLY BY LAURIE WEISSGARBER

You said you loved me
With all your heart;
That never again
Would we be apart.
But look at us now,
So different and strange'
Who would have ever thought
We both would change.
But I want you to know
That from the beginning,
The love we felt never died,
But just kept fading.
And that faded love
I hold dearly in my heart;
For it's given me strength
Since we've been apart.
I thank you
For the time we shared,
And through everything that's happened

POSSIBLY BY LAURIE WEISSGARBER

I always knew you cared.
So you see my love,
We changed so much with each new day,
That the love we felt never died;
It just faded away.

LOVE

AUGUST 17TH, 1989, HYDE PARK, NEW YORK

    Today was one of the happiest days of my life. I went for a checkup and I found out that I am pregnant. I felt like a butterfly floating on air. I have always wanted to be a mommy. Now it's coming true!!

    After I left my doctor's I drove home with a big smile on my face; also yelling "I am going to be a mommy!"

    I was so happy I cried for joy! ♡

— LAURIE WEISSGARBER

90

LOVE IS....

POSSIBLY BY LAURIE WEISSGARBER

Little things you could do to make people
 happy.
Often saying I love you for being you.
Very special person
Even in good times and bad times.

Drawn by Laurie at bottom of poem

91

LOVE (1)

POSSIBLY BY LAURIE WEISSGARBER

Love is the smile of a friend,
A helping hand
Or when someone says,
"I understand."
It's that compliment you give
When someone's feeling sad,
Or that bit of advice
When troubles come on bad.
It's the touch of a hand,
But most of all,
It's helping out someone
When they feel small.

92

LOVE (2)

UNKNOWN AUTHOR

Love is a signature engraved
deeply on your heart,
Written in a special ink with long and
lasting art.
Monogrammed with trust and care,
a sweet and tender rhyme
Outlined with a familiar smile and
memories of time.
Love is a dream you dream
sometimes when your mind
can ease the pain,
A day dream of sunshine in the sky
when all you see is rain,
A thought of being together,
knowing someone's there
A wish for laughs and happiness,
enough to give and share.
Love is an image of how you feel and
what you want to be,
A reflection on the way you live and

UNKNOWN AUTHOR

what you like to see.
A picture you paint of yourself and
the things you like to do,
An impression left about the ones
that mean so much to you.

93

LOVE (3)

UNKNOWN AUTHOR

Love is like the wind.
You can't see or touch it,
But it's always there.
It can lift you up
Or bring you down.
And it's sure to turn
Your world around.

94

I ASK MYSELF

UNKNOWN AUTHOR

I ask myself
Why I have been
Blessed with someone
So understanding
And so caring...
Perhaps it's because,
I can truly appreciate you
Or maybe it's because
God knew
I need you
So much.

95

THINKING OF YOU (2)

UNKNOWN AUTHOR

Let me think of you
With a smile in my heart.
I want to remember the good times,
Not the bad.
When my tear-filled eyes
Take on the beauty of the stars
I'll think of you
For my first love is too special
To remember with pain.

96

MAKE IT UP

UNKNOWN AUTHOR

Life is too short for grievances —
For quarrels and for tears,
What's the use of wasting
Precious days and precious tears.
If there's something to forgive —
Forgive without delay —
Maybe you too, were part to blame,
So make it up today,
Be generous–forget the past
And take the broader view,
Cast away all bitterness and
Let the sun shine through.
If it's within your power
A broken heart to mend,
Remember — Love is all that
Really matters — in the end.

97

YOU

UNKNOWN AUTHOR

You bring a smile to my face
You make my heart race
You are the rainbow in my sky
You are my one and only guy!

98

NEVER BLIND

POSSIBLY BY LAURIE WEISSGARBER

True love is so hard to find
But when it finally is found
It is never blind.
Instead it brings an added light
From which to see the inner beauties
Hidden deep from common sight.

99

COLORFUL GOOD-BYES

UNKNOWN AUTHOR

As the cool night breeze blows through the
    window,
I see in the distant sky
The blue and pink of the sun that's left us today
And said it's colorful good-byes.
It reminds me of nights before,
Filled with love and tender moments.
It was a young, innocent romance
That flowered into sweet understanding.
But young we were,
Too vulnerable and trusting.
Our love we had so treasured
Grew faded and dusty.
We parted with no tears or regret of any kind.
Just a pearl of emptiness in our hearts.
And a garden of forget-me-nots in our minds.

100

LOVE (4)

POSSIBLY BY LAURIE WEISSGARBER

Let it grow, openly
Open your heart, tenderly,
Verify your feelings, you and he,
Expect no more than what you know can be.

101

A WISH COME TRUE

UNKNOWN AUTHOR

Of all my wishes only one has come true,
The wonderful wish of being loved by you.
You've shown me happiness far beyond end
Since we've become more than "just friends".
When I'm with you my spirits soar,
With each passing day I love you more.
When I gaze into your eyes and see them glisten,
I sit quiet and just let my heart listen.
'Cause sometimes your look is all it takes
To make my heart flutter and my hands shake.
So when others say its useless to wish upon a
    star,
Now I can tell them how wrong they are.

102

WHAT ARE THESE FEELINGS
UNKNOWN AUTHOR

My tongue gets all tied,
My knees start to shiver,
My body gets woozy,
My teeth start to quiver,
I start to breathe heavy,
My heart starts to pound,
I try to talk
But I can't make a sound.
When I see you in the distance
I always seem to stare,
Imagine how I feel
When you are near.
Night after night,
I ask the stars above,
Could this great feeling
Really be love?

103

SPECIAL FEELINGS

POSSIBLY BY LAURIE WEISSGARBER

When you hold me in your arms,
The whole world stops
And waits for you to let go.
But you don't.
You keep holding me and loving me
Until the world begins to turn again,
Revolving around our love.

104

TOGETHER

UNKNOWN AUTHOR

You're my one and only love
And this I want you to know
You mean more to me than anything,
I don't ever want you to go.
Loving you gives me happiness,
The kind I need each day.
And if sometimes I don't show it,
I love you in each and every way.
If sometimes I get jealous,
It's only because I care.
The love I feel of you,
Is ever so rare.
If I could have one wish
Do you know what it would be?
For us to be together
For all eternity.

105

ONCE IN A LIFETIME

UNKNOWN AUTHOR

Just once in lifetime
The right one comes along
The feeling is immortal,
To know you belong.
Just once in a lifetime,
You see his honest face,
You touch his loving hand,
You feel his warm embrace.
Just once in a lifetime
Everything feels right.
You see his shining face
And your darkness turns to light.
Just once in a lifetime
The feeling is so new,
To say three words
And mean them,
The words are
I LOVE YOU!

106

FORGET ME NOT

UNKNOWN AUTHOR

Our new-found love was exciting and fun.
We shared ourselves, telling of all we'd done.
In our closeness, our lives were fused together
With promise to remain together, forever.
But I realized, as we grew with time,
That you could never fully be mine.
Our lives were too different in the past.
Our future together would never last.
Now I know we must lead our lives a part,
While keeping fond memories close to heart.
Please treasure our love with each passing day
It helped us to grow in a special way.
Like the tiny flower that wilts and dies.
My fading love for you also cries,
"Forget me not."
Remember me always with smiles and gladness
Regret not our meeting, with tears and sadness.
For if you feel sad at times of recall
I'd rather you remember me never at all.

Forget Me Not

But like the tiny flower that wilts and dies,
My fading love for you also cries,
"Forget me not."

107

A FRIEND IS AMIE

UNKNOWN AUTHOR

Friend —
A seeming mirror of myself,
And I, of you.
My shadow, my other half, my confidante,
And I, yours.
So alike that I often wonder –
If we hadn't lived at the same time,
At the same place,
And fate had not fancied our meeting,
Would we not feel that something –
A piece of ourselves –
Was missing?
Or perhaps that we, in turn,
Should be part of someone else?
I am a puzzle with one piece missing.
You are my missing piece.
Sometimes I wish to be you –
And you, me.
Because we are so different

A Friend Is Amie

We have so much to share –
Because we are so alike,
We understand each other so well.

108

LIVING IN THE PAST

UNKNOWN AUTHOR

I find myself
Living in the past
Holding on to a love
That did not last.
Always dreaming of you
And the times that we shared
Back when you were here
To show me you cared.
But now you're gone
And deep down I know
That maybe I should
Just let you go.
I would if only
I could find a way
To stop living in the past
And start living today.

109

MR. TRUE LOVE

POSSIBLY BY LAURIE WEISSGARBER

A true love doesn't care if you're short or tall
He doesn't care if you forget to call.
He loves to talk and is always there to hear
Your happiness, sadness, your dreams and fears.
Don't be impatient cause there are many fakes.
If you want him, you'll wait the time it takes.
So go and seek your lover true,
Don't whine, be sad or very blue.
For one day you'll try, turn around, and see
A wonderful person, your true love to be.

110

SHINING

UNKNOWN AUTHOR

I did not ask for
bouquets of roses,
candle lit dinners, or,
walks in the moonlight
Because
roses wilt,
candles burn out, and
the moon goes down.
I asked for your love
Because love is forever
growing,
burning and
shining.

111

LET LOVE GROW

UNKNOWN AUTHOR

Love is like a flower,
So let it bloom.
Once you plant your seed
Give it room,
Talk to it with understanding
And not with doubt.
Water it slowly and you'll see it sprout.
Let your smile reflect the sun's rays.
Let the stern grow stronger, day by day,
Be gentle, be patient and take it slow.
And you will see how beautiful
Your love will grow.

112

THE PERFECT LOVE

UNKNOWN AUTHOR

You whisper in my ear
You gently touch my cheek,
You help me, oh, so quietly
To find the things I seek
You're there when I celebrate
And when I feel blue,
It seems you're always at my side
We're like one, not two.
You guide me ever so patiently
With tender loving care,
It seems that you were made for me
We are a perfect pair.
You know my moods, and I know yours.
Together our love will grow,
To find a world of happiness
That everyone should know.
Our love will never die
I know that this is true,
'Cause every time I see you
I fall in a new.

113

LOVE (5)

UNKNOWN AUTHOR

Something inside me
Is twisting and turning.
My heart is thumping,
Burning and yearning.
It's hard to explain.
Yet it's pleasant and comforting,
Leaving no sorrow or pain.
Something is calling
From far above,
Telling me,
….that something is **Love**!

114

LOVE (6)

UNKNOWN AUTHOR

Love is blind
Until you see
How much love
There is to be!

115

TRUE LOVE

UNKNOWN AUTHOR

My heart is full
Of love for him
And all his caring ways
I'm set adrift
Upon an ocean
High majestic
Atop a wave
My throne is the sea
And my court the gulls
That dance through my kingdom.
The sun it sets
With brilliant colors,
The stars above
Shine on and on
To show my endless reign
Upon the throne
Of my love
Never to come down again.

116

LOVE (7)

UNKNOWN AUTHOR

Love is like a flower ready to bloom.
It comes from deep inside.
It is something that warms the heart.
It brings out something special between two people.
Love is like a seagull flying free,
Being high on emotions.
Putting his worries out of his mind
And just letting his emotions soar.

117

THE MYSTERY OF LOVE

UNKNOWN AUTHOR

Love makes you feel special. It changes everyone for the better. It is the one commodity that multiples when you give it away. The more you spread it around, the more you are able to hang on to it because it keeps coming back to you. Where love is concerned, it pays to be an absolute spendthrift. It cannot be bought nor sold, so give it away! Throw it away! Splash it all over! Empty your pockets! Shake the basket! Turn it upside down! Shower it on everyone — even those who don't deserve it! You may startle them into behaving in a way you never dreamed possible. Not only is it the sweet mystery of life, it is the most powerful motivator known to humankind.

118

FAR AWAY THOUGHTS

UNKNOWN AUTHOR

Since the day I first met you
My life has really changed
Some things I put in order,
Some things I've rearranged.
I've put you in the middle
And built my dreams around
Someone who means so much to me,
The special one I've found
Before you came into my life
My skies were not as blue
But then one day you came along
And the sun came shining through.
Although we may be far apart,
The miles cannot erase
The precious memories that I have
Of pretty blue eyes and smiling face.
So now I'm waiting patiently
For the day when you'll come home.
I'll not regret one moment spent

Far Away Thoughts

Of reminiscing while you're gone.
Some say you're where your thoughts are,
Now if that thought is true,
You don't ever have to be lonely,
For I'll always be with you.

119

NOT TO TOUCH

UNKNOWN AUTHOR

I close my eyes and there you are,
As sudden as day breaks and night falls.
I reach out to touch you,
You're not there, but only in my mind.
I can't have you there every moment,
To tell you how much I care bout you
Or to put my arms around you and hold you
    tight.
At times I only wish you
To be there by my side.
For you to need me as all need you.
I want to be close to you,
But since I can't, I'll continue
Closing my eyes, finding you there,
As sudden as day breaks and night falls,
But not to touch.

120

NEXT TIME

UNKNOWN AUTHOR

Now he's gone
But I'm not gonna cry,
I say to myself
While wiping my eye.
We never had a chance,
We never got to try.
But what hurts most of all
Is I never got to say good-bye.
For awhile I blamed you,
I said you were too shy.
But now that you're gone I realize
That so was I.
I should've made the first move,
Not left it up to chance.
I was afraid of being rejected,
But I might have found romance.
Well now I've learned my lesson,
Next time I'm gonna try.
The heck with old traditions –
Why can't a girl ask out a guy?

121

HIDDEN LOVE

UNKNOWN AUTHOR

The most painful type of love there is
Is love that's left unknown.
A love that cannot be expressed,
Affection left unknown,
It's a love that hides behind a mask
Of happiness and glee.
Yet all that's left down deep inside
Is pain and misery.
It's love that tries to hideaway
How much it really cares.
It keeps locked within its heart
The feeling flowing there.
This love withholds touching,
Afraid of what it would say,
And the most painful thing about hidden love
Is that it never fades away.

122

YOU ONLY HAVE TO SAY "HELLO"
POSSIBLY BY LAURIE WEISSGARBER

You only have to say "Hello"
And instantly I find
My heart is filled with smiles of joy —
My cares are far behind...
You only have to say "Hello"
And suddenly I feel
A special glow inside of me
So very warm and real...
And when I need the morning sun
To start my day off right
You only have to say "Hello"
and life is sweet and bright...

123

VALENTINE'S DAY

POSSIBLY BY LAURIE WEISSGARBER

This Valentine's Day
Not unlike the ones already past,
You search for the love
You hope will last.
Every time you see him,
That very special guy,
Your hope this year Cupid
Will land the bull's eye.
You have to let your feelings loose,
Give that special guy a chance.
For if you do and he responds,
It could be the start of a new romance.
For this Valentine's Day
Think up a little scheme,
You can take the initiative
And not just dream.
This February 14th
Don't let him pass you by,
Put on your nicest smile
And begin with a simple "Hi!"

124

YOUR LOVE

POSSIBLY BY LAURIE WEISSGARBER

Hidden dreams
Never revealed,
Broken hearts
Never healed.
Lost friends
Never found,
Helping hands
Never around.
Quiet smiles
Never heard,
Unspoken thoughts
Never a word.
Your love
Never felt
My heart
Forever melts.

DREAMS

MAY 5TH, 1989 5:20 PM, HYDE PARK, NEW YORK

These are my dreams:

1. Donate $25,000 to Gannett House's Child Care program so that they could...have a block + art room, and a library!!!!
2. Open my own Daycare Center
3. Go on a vacation to Disney World, Australia, and France
4. Have a reunion with all the children I took care of at GH
5. Buy a nice boat so I could go waterskiing
6. Go to Norway with Grandpa, which is his homeland
7. That my grandpa & grandmothers live to see my first child

— LAURIE WEISSGARBER

Editor's Note: Many of Laurie's 1989 dreams came true. She owned and ran Sunshine daycare in the early '90s, visited Disney World with her children, and while she never traveled overseas, her eldest son visited Australia & France. No known reunion occurred. Though she never owned a boat, she often kayaked with her husband, Steve. Her grandparents lived to see her first child. Her dream of donating to childcare was realized through a lifetime of work in childcare and volunteering for Make-A-Wish.

125

ESCAPE

POSSIBLY BY LAURIE WEISSGARBER

With a flip of a page
I am transported to a world
Where my deepest fantasies come true.
A world of paper and print
And imagination.
I lose myself
In this fantasy,
Oblivious to all else
Until, reluctantly,
The last page is turned
And I inevitably
Must return
To reality.

126

REALITY

CARRIE J. MYERS

Upon a star,
Wishing.
In the dark of night,
Dreaming.
At break of dawn,
Drifting
Toward reality.
In light of day,
Creating
Imperfect image
Of the dream.
Oh, where has fled
The fugitive gleam
Of paradise – the dream?
Night remembers
Joyful sleep
Where dream are
Reality.

127

SOMETIME...

UNKNOWN AUTHOR

I watch the sun come up
And I realize that I have another day
To work toward my ambitions,
Sometimes...
I watch the sun go down
And I realize that I am a day older,
A day wiser,
And a step closer to my dreams.
Some day...
I will reflect on these quiet times;
Glad that I wondered,
Glad that I took the time to feel.
For every great accomplishment
Starts with a glimmer of hope,
And a small dream dreamt.

128

ALL YOU CAN BE

UNKNOWN AUTHOR

Miracles can happen
Dreams can come true
If you have faith in
All that you do.
Believe in yourself
And you will see
That with faith
You will be all you can be.

129

IMAGINATION

UNKNOWN AUTHOR

Awesome is the power of imagination
For it shapes our lives
Builds our dreams
And
Leaves our minds to wander.

130

TAKE A CHANCE

UNKNOWN AUTHOR

Every person has hidden goals and dreams.
Often people are afraid to reach for what
    gleams.
Afraid of being ridiculed or failing,
Never reaching cloud nine,
Laughing and sailing.
Don't ignore that need inside,
It will grow.
Though you may try to make it hide.
One shouldn't always, do what is expected.
You must take the chance,
Of being rejected.
Taking a chance often leads to some pairs

131

DREAMS

UNKNOWN AUTHOR

When the days are long and dreary,
And the nights only seem to make one weary,
Dreams and fantasies can fulfill
And give life strength and will.
Yet the same dreams that carry one on.
Can cause pain and suffering beyond,
If carried to the point where they become,
A substitute for the life of days to come.

132

DREAM YOUR LIFE AWAY
POSSIBLY BY LAURIE WEISSGARBER

Dreams are what life is made of,
But don't get carried away.
Work to make them happen,
Every single day.
You can't get through life
With just a simple dream.
Although it may sound fun,
It's not as easy as it seems.
So don't keep dreaming,
You have to work hard every day.
Make your dream a reality,
Don't dream your life away.

133

ALL THAT'S WISHED FOR YOU

POSSIBLY BY LAURIE WEISSGARBER

Pause awhile to think about
The sunniest of days —
Think in terms of spending time
In all your favorite ways...
Imagine happy moments
In the company of friends
Enjoying all the laughter
That the brightest lifetime sends...
Add to this, the finest health,
Your best dreams come true
And you won't have to guess all
What's being wished of you...

134

HOLD ON TO YOUR DREAMS

UNKNOWN AUTHOR

Hold on to your dreams.
Don't ever give in
If you keep trying
You're going to win.
Hold on to your dreams.
Though sometimes it's hard
Just hold your head up
And reach for the stars.
Hold on to your dreams.
Though they seem far away
Those dreams will come true.
Somehow — some way!

135

TO HAVE A DREAM

UNKNOWN AUTHOR

Always have a dream and believe
it will come true.
Strive to make it happen
in everything you do.
For dreams are what
make life worth living.
Love worth taking and
love worth giving.
Dreams keep life
from being boring.
They lift up your spirit
and keep it soaring.

ART

Books can change our lives. When I was a young child I loved to read Little House on the Prairie, The Hardy Boys, Nancy Drew, and others. But I would get frustrated because I read slowly and wanted to get all the details of the story—which made me not read as much. As I got older and became an adult, I again enjoyed reading many, many stories to young children at my job; and books for pleasure about couples and other topics.

People can learn a lot from their books. I like books that give you ideas about organizing your storage space. I used the book "School Before Six" to get ideas for my nursery school class. I liked reading "Passages" in my free time. There is one book that I truly loved, Walk Across America.

— LAURIE WEISSGARBER

136

WHAT MUSIC CAN DO

POSSIBLY BY LAURIE WEISSGARBER

You flip the switch,
And turn the dial.
Then you sit
And listen awhile.
The beat picks up,
The music blares.
You're goin crazy,
And everyone stares.
You're having fun
As you jump around
You look about
And what have you found?
The whole room has gotten up
To join in with you
Now you know
What music can do!

137
THROUGH AN ARTIST'S EYES
UNKNOWN AUTHOR

Through an artist's eyes
Life can be full of surprise.
Every little thing of interest
He can relate on canvas.
Whether it's purple and red, big or small,
Black and white, short or tall.
Life takes on a colorful meaning,
Reality and fantasy are worth believing.
The truth of life never dies
When it's looked at
Through an artist's eyes.

138

ARTIST ANONYMOUS

POSSIBLY BY LAURIE WEISSGARBER

We are all artists
Day after day
Painting life's picture
Sad or gay.
When I was a child
There were only a few colors
Each new experience
Added another.
On life's canvas so big
My brush will I take
And begin today's picture
Right when I wake.
A stroke of the brush
Is every smile or tear
A bright thought or dim
Is gray sky or clear.
Let joy be your song
And your brush will release
A rainbow of beauty,
A masterpiece.

OCEAN

I went on a whale watch [in September 1990]. It was so exciting. We went a very long way out to the ocean to look for whales. We were lucky, we saw fin whales, no humpbacks. The whales swam right near the boat.

— LAURIE WEISSGARBER

139

THE SEA (1)

BY LAURIE WEISSGARBER

The sea is like a wonderland of beauty and charm.
The sea is more beautiful than any land.
The sea glitters like diamonds
When the sun shines on it.
The sea is like a whole new place
Where you can relax and enjoy
It's quietness and loneliness.
The sea is a lovely place
It's so quiet and peaceful!
It's a place for lovers.
So they can be with each other.
The sea can be a charming place.
But you have to love the sea
To enjoy its beauty.
Go boating sometime
And you will see for yourself
How beautiful and lovely it really is!

140

AN OCEAN OF FEELINGS

POSSIBLY BY LAURIE WEISSGARBER

The stillness of the night haunts me.
I can feel the coldness of the waves
Crashing at my feet.
Though it's hard to let go of my feelings for you,
I let the tide take my pain
And wait for the sunrise to bring a new day.

141

REFLECTIONS (2)

POSSIBLY BY LAURIE WEISSGARBER

You made me smile
With your
Strange, different way of
Talking,
Acting,
Putting up a front,
Being tough when you were unsure
Of yourself; funny
To think of you being unsure.
Some say I should hate you for
Things you did; funny
To think of me hating you.
It would be the last thing
I would ever do.

142

SEA SHELL

POSSIBLY BY LAURIE WEISSGARBER

I go to the beach
Early in the morning
And watch the tide come in.
The blue rushing waters
Swallow the sand
And go back out again.
This time they carry in
A sea shell —
I pick it up,
So small and smooth,
A pink coral color
So intimately beautiful.
I put it back on the sand
And the waves carry it away.
Created in the sea,
And in the sea it will stay,
Until another young girl
Picks it up
And marvels at its beauty.

143

THE BEACH

POSSIBLY BY LAURIE WEISSGARBER

The beach is my favorite sight,
And very beautiful at night.
The way the waves jump and dance,
And bring the promise of romance.
The sand is warm beneath my feet,
A great place for two people to meet.
A sunset is the greatest sight,
And if you've seen one,
You'll know,
I'm right.

144

MYSTERIOUS SURFER

POSSIBLY BY LAURIE WEISSGARBER

Lying in the summer sun,
Waiting, hoping for some fun.
Cute surfer catches my eye
As he saunters right on by.
I follow him with my gaze,
Soon he's lost in the haze.
Later on in the day
I'm just walking on my way,
When there he is, my surfer boy,
Causing by, looking coy.
His eyes look right into mine,
I keep hoping for some sign.
On his way he finally goes,
Who he is, I may never know.

145

THE SEA (2)

POSSIBLY BY LAURIE WEISSGARBER

The sea is like
Man
Pushing full force ahead
Then
Rushing back

146

THE OCEAN (1)

UNKNOWN AUTHOR

Each wave races another,
With the edge of the land
It's finish line.
Each wave acting as one human being;
Setting a mark for itself,
A goal,
And fighting to fulfill it.

147

SEASIDE MOMENTS

UNKNOWN AUTHOR

Tingling mist upon my face
Cool refreshing salty taste.
Gentle lapping of sea so green
Melancholy aura, so serene.
Screeching, squawk of gulls on high
Searching, diving, soaring by.
Distant puffs of white so wide
Seemingly close to wondering eyes.

148

THE OCEAN (2)

UNKNOWN AUTHOR

The warmth of the sun
Quickly heats me
As wave upon wave
Envelopes me in its foam.
A sense of isolation,
Beautiful solitude.
Creeps over me,
As my half-closed eyes sleepily witness
The fleecy clouds drifting by.
The roar of the sea keeps me awake
Yet puts my mind to sleep to
All its troubles.
With an interminable song,
Days could pass, even weeks,
And I would stay here,
For the complete, serene peacefulness,
This bliss,
Is how life should be.

149

THE SEA (3)

UNKNOWN AUTHOR

The waves crash against the shore.
The seagulls cry the warning of the storm.
The fishermen come in from a day's work with
    their catch.
And the painter's start to sketch the dark
    clouded sky.

150

MEETING AT NIGHT

ROBERT BROWNING

The grey sea and the long black land;
    And the yellow half moon large and low;
    And the startled little waves that leap
    In fiery ringlets from their sleep,
    As I gain the cove with pushing prow,
    And quench its speed in the slushy sand.

THEN A MILE OF WARM, sea-scented beach;
    Three fields to cross till a farm appears;
    A tap at the pane, The quick sharp scratch
    And blue spurt of a lighted match,
    And a voiceless bud, through its joy and fears,
    Than the two hearts beating each to each!

151

THE OCEAN (3)

POSSIBLY BY LAURIE WEISSGARBER

All alone I sit,
No one around,
Above me
The lonely echo
Of the seagull.
I look out far
Into the massive stretch
Of unknown depths
Before me.
I know beneath
The surface
Is a quiet world
That belongs to me.
As I wait, I watch
The surf pounding
Against the sand.
All around is solitude
And I can feel the intimacy
Between us.
When I come here

POSSIBLY BY LAURIE WEISSGARBER

I talk...
To the wind
The sand
The ocean...
And I know I
Have been with
Friends.

152

OCEAN ROMANCE

UNKNOWN AUTHOR

Moonlight falls across the sea
The white-capped waves tumble silently.
The sailing wind whispers through the trees
Romance is found on an ocean breeze.
The sand underneath many bare feet,
Is quick to detect a racing heartbeat.
Tiny animals that roam the ground
Miss not a secret, overlook not a sound.
The heavens above and waves that dance
Are wise to the happenings of an ocean
    romance.

NATURE

Waterfalls are so beautiful and carefree feeling. I love nature and the outdoors. The woods are so nice and quiet.

I will always remember my adventures finding all the waterfalls I could.

— LAURIE WEISSGARBER

153

THE SANDS OF TIME

UNKNOWN AUTHOR

Lightly step the golden stars
Around their celestial sphere,
Shimmering waves of northern lights
Might suddenly appear.
A hunter's moon with an earthly glow
Will soon become old lore.
This radiant splendor of the skies,
As ships are called to shore,
Fades away in the early morn'
Only to return once more.

154

CLOUDS

POSSIBLY BY LAURIE WEISSGARBER

A cloud stands like cotton
on a blue sky
Like a scoop of vanilla ice cream
on a blueberry pie
Like a marshmallow toasting
on a sapphire flame
A white velvet sea....a cloud
Is its name.

155

FREE FLIGHT

POSSIBLY BY LAURIE WEISSGARBER

Free like the wind
And soaring high
Sometimes I'd like to be
A butterfly.
Yes, I love you
And you love me.
But once in awhile
I need to be free.
To soar on my dreams
And reach for the sky,
Just like the beautiful
Little butterfly.
So, just for today
Let me be free
To chase my own rainbows
And celebrate me.
I'll never forget our love
And our happy times together.
I'll cherish what we had

POSSIBLY BY LAURIE WEISSGARBER

Now and forever.
So free like the wind
And soaring high
Yes, just for today
I am a butterfly.

156

THINKING OF YOU (3)

POSSIBLY BY LAURIE WEISSGARBER

Think of golden sunbeams
And morning in the sky,
Think of apple blossoms,
And blue birds flying by,
Think of quiet pathways
And dancing mountain streams,
Think of sleepy valleys
And rainbows painting dreams,
Think of hidden meadows
Where happy robins sing
And you'll have some idea
What each thought of you can bring

157

SUNSET

UNKNOWN AUTHOR

Blue, pink, orange and purple
Weave themselves together
In a spectacular array
Of the last fleeting moments
Of the day.
Blue waves to pink as
Orange and purple dance,
Playing tricks with the sun.
Then finally, the beautiful colors surrender
To the night
As the stars say "hello".

158

DON'T RUSH IN

POSSIBLY BY LAURIE WEISSGARBER

Sea shells hold the special song
Of the love that just somehow went wrong.
The moon has told a thousand lies
That turned hellos into good-bye.
The sea has cried a thousand tears
For loves that fade through the years.
The breeze has brought back
faded dreams of the past.
The dreams of those who were in a hurry
and went too fast.
And if the stars could talk –
Oh, if only the stars could talk –
They'd tell you that before you run
You first must learn to walk.

159

I'D LIKE TO BE A BIRD

UNKNOWN AUTHOR

I'd like to be a bird
Soaring through the air;
With the wind flowing
Through my wings
I'd glide over the ocean,
The world subsiding
Below.

Illustration created from four individual drawings by Laurie Jean

160

BEFORE THE DOWNPOUR

UNKNOWN AUTHOR

The clouds hung heavy and low
Giving a depressing look to the day;
A great cloth blotting out the sun.
The thick heat was broken only now
And then by the slightest
Semblance of a breeze.
The water lay still as the animals did.
The atmosphere was electric —
The pause notable.
Then the downpour began.

161

THE KITE

POSSIBLY BY LAURIE WEISSGARBER

I had a kite that flew so high,
Way, way up in the sky.
Then one day the string slipped out of my hand,
Away it flew, up over the land,
As I watched it fly so high,
All I could do was let out a sigh.
It was free, free as the wind,
I watched it glide and watched it bend.
It flew over cities and over the sea,
It flew over an island and got caught high in a
    tree,
And I'm sorry to say
That's probably where it will stay.

162

THE STARS

POSSIBLY BY LAURIE WEISSGARBER

The stars, how they twinkle so bright,
How they shine during the dark, empty night.
They glow for everyone to see;
I watch as they smile and twinkle at me.
I love to watch a falling star –
Watch it fly very far.
It gracefully soars through the sky,
Like a huge airplane passing by.
The stars — how they twinkle so bright,
How they shine during the darkness of the
    night.

163

SHOOTING STARS

POSSIBLY BY LAURIE WEISSGARBER

I must live before I die,
A shooting star darts across the sky.
Gliding swiftly through the night,
Moving toward the guiding light.
Shining brightly as the sun,
Two stars together move as one.
It is one star, the star is us,
As against each galaxy we brush.
Holding hands to join the glow,
As two we falter, best as one we grow.
Burning with our own sweet fire,
Soaring together, higher, and higher.

164

GRACE

UNKNOWN AUTHOR

The gracefulness of nature
Whispers poetry
To all who will listen...
Stirring feelings
Of reverence...
Awakening hearts
To a sense of the sublime.

165

SANCTUARY

UNKNOWN AUTHOR

In the soothing stillness of a place apart,
We see more fully,
Hear more clearly,
Feel more deeply
The earth's gentle secrets.

166

LIVING TREASURES

UNKNOWN AUTHOR

In a bold display
Of splendor,
Nature reveals
Her living treasures...
Inspiring us to recognize
The intricate wonder
Of all creation.

167

THE OLD OAK TREE

POSSIBLY BY LAURIE WEISSGARBER

I wonder how long it's been standing there,
So quietly and with great dignity.
What stories it could tell
If only it could talk to me.
How many people have enjoyed its shade.
And carved their initials along its face?
How many children played among its limbs.
Or used it as a meeting place?
I wonder if the birds and squirrels there now
Worry about its history.
I wish I knew the answer to these questions,
But to me they remain a mystery.

168

HARMONY

UNKNOWN AUTHOR

When we take time
To savor the fullness of life...
To reflect on the harmony
Of nature...
We begin to realize
Our kinship
With all the earth.

169

SINCE THE SUNRISE

POSSIBLY BY LAURIE WEISSGARBER

Since the sunrise,
Day has come.
It opens hearts and minds for some.
For others it is only light,
The opposite of dark and night.
But he who sees a sunrise
And never sees the rain,
Will never see the loss
And only see the gain.
For a sunrise is a memory,
A treasure there to hold.
You must listen to its music,
For a secret will unfold.

170

SMALL WONDER

POSSIBLY BY LAURIE WEISSGARBER

Lovely and lush,
You stand straight and tall
So different from brush –
A wonder so small.
You sway in the breeze,
You just carry on
Upon the lawn.
You are grass.

SEASONS

I think that childhood is the best time in life. Children don't have to worry about money and having a job. Childhood is a time to run free and enjoy the outdoors.

— LAURIE WEISSGARBER

171

SPRING BREEZES

POSSIBLY BY LAURIE WEISSGARBER

I like to feel the spring breezes
That blow so fresh and free.
I like to feel them tassel my hair
And push and at me.
They rush among the budding trees
And kiss the early grass.
And make the tulips bow to them
In greeting as they pass.

172

SPRING IS NEAR

CARRIE J. MYERS

Flowers bloom with a scent that delights
Soft pink blossoms, what a lovely sight
Meadows brim with tall, green grass
A lovely sight for all who pass
Warm, bright days filled with cheer
For everyone knows, spring is here.

173

CELEBRATION

UNKNOWN AUTHOR

As our senses awaken
To the season's
Unfolding glory,
We breathe
The richly scented
Newness of a fine,
Fair day
And celebrate
It's dawning
With our wonder.

174

BEAUTIFUL THINGS

UNKNOWN AUTHOR

Mountains so high,
Flowers that bloom,
Birds that fly,
The shining moon.
A walk in the park
On a warm summer day,
The dogs that bark,
Little children at play.
The pretty, golden sun
That shines so bright,
It shines on everyone
As nature's own light.
These are the things
That are beautiful to me —
What nature brings
For everyone to see.

175

SUMMER VISIONS

POSSIBLY BY LAURIE WEISSGARBER

Smoke curling up from once-burning coals.
The sweet, fragrant scent of the garden's red rose,
The smell of the afternoon's mowing lingers in the air,
Laughter and cotton candy promises from a neighborhood fair.
Sprinkler's droplets glisten in the grass —
Summer visions echo and begin to fade
Reflected in the prisms of a snowflake.

176

SUMMER DREAMS (2)

UNKNOWN AUTHOR

As I searched for sea treasures
I could hold in my hands,
Remembering past walks along these sands.
Not a thought did I give
To the dreams in my heart
For I was saying my goodbyes
To those dreams I have outgrown,
And to those cast out to the sea
Maybe to be found by a girl
Waiting to grow into a woman,
Perhaps not unlike me.

177

SUMMER'S END

UNKNOWN AUTHOR

Sailboat silhouettes glide
Across the misty horizon
Flocks of seagulls cry in anguish
And disappear in the gray sky
Cold sand is hard beneath my bare feet
As I walk down miles
Of endless beach
A fog horn echoes
The mist turns to rain.

178

I AM AUTUMN

UNKNOWN AUTHOR

The candied breath of fall sweeps a street
And tugs at leaves of weeping trees.
Romance is felt in crisp, fresh air.
The bittersweet season is new and fair.
The autumn gusts send a chill
For one short moment
Then all is still.
The mass of luminescence we call sun
Is concealed by clouds —
A frightened one.
All at once the clouds blow by
The sun's again allowed to shine.
The amber, crimson and rusty whirl
Is laid to rest —
A sleepy girl.
The end of summer, her moods are ranging.
She is like me —
I'm always changing.

179

FINDING NATURE

UNKNOWN AUTHOR

I walk with myself
On a chilled fall afternoon
Befriending nature.
Beside a still lake
I escape reality —
And enter wonderland.
As if glass,
The water displays a life
Which I dream about.
Our world in water.
One tremendous reflection
Finally peaceful.

180

GOLDEN

UNKNOWN AUTHOR

Golden is the morning sun
That shines forth through the day.
Golden is your loving touch,
Your soft and gentle way.
Golden is a shining star
That makes your dreams come true.
Golden is the falling leaf
A sky of autumn blue.
So when you're in a winter world
And everything is cold,
Just close your eyes and dream your dreams
And your thoughts will turn to gold.

181

WINTER

UNKNOWN AUTHOR

The skies are gray, the ground is white,
The winter's grin brings forth delight
To those who live the silent snow
And roaring winds that blow and blow.
And when one looks outside, one sees,
The nakedness of lonely trees.
All living creatures run and hide.
Queen Winter's rule begins outside.
She wears her icy crown with ease,
Her stinging glances quickly freeze
Small lakes and rivers, pools and falls.
Her servant winds she loudly calls,
They come and gladly help conceal
The warmth one often longs to feel.
When flowers bloom and skies are clear,
When grass is green and summer's near.
But don't despair, when some months pass,
The snow will melt, revealing grass.
The rainbows will be seen again,
The Princess Spring will come to reign.

OTHER

I enjoy working with children because they are so much fun to play with and talk to. They love to tell you all about their pets and about what they did on the weekend. Children at my job like to tell me about what they got for Christmas and what they got for their birthdays. Working with children is rewarding to me because they always make me smile or laugh.

— LAURIE WEISSGARBER

182

AGE

POSSIBLY BY LAURIE WEISSGARBER

Some people are fooled by a person's age.
They might think that the person is older or younger.
When you are younger, you are happy about your age,
And you celebrate your birthday.
When you get older you are afraid to have your birthday,
Because who wants to get old and get gray hairs.

183

GOOD OL' SNOOPY

POSSIBLY BY LAURIE WEISSGARBER

Oh, you're so cute,
I love you so.
For you're a dog
Who steals the show.
Your floppy ears,
Your sweet, sly grin
Make me feel good within.
Your friends are human,
Your pal is a bird.
You understand him —
I don't catch a word!
As you grow
Older and more clever,
Remember, we love you
More than ever!

184

MODERN WORLD

POSSIBLY BY LAURIE WEISSGARBER

What's happened to shyness and acting natural?
    To hearts beating fast and driving
    each other crazy without even touching?
    To desire, to respect —
    Did they die out with black-and-white TV?

185

THE LITTLE MERMAID

POSSIBLY BY LAURIE WEISSGARBER

She wears a crown of seashells
upon her silken hair,
And dances with the towering waves
without a single care.
At night she sits upon a rock
to watch the velvet sky,
And from this little mermaid
you hear a tiny sigh.

186

TIME

UNKNOWN AUTHOR

Time....
Gentle sculptor
Of the earth
And of our lives....
Delicately shaping
Our brightest dreams
Into beautiful realities.

187

ENCHANTMENT

UNKNOWN AUTHOR

Within the heart
Of every lovely thing
Enchantment waits...
To carry us
Beyond the everyday
To a timeless world....
Of joy.

188

MIRACLES

UNKNOWN AUTHOR

Miracles lie within miracles...
Transcending all we know
Of life's reality...
Offering us a glimpse
Of true perfection
To treasure for all time.

189

I WANT

UNKNOWN AUTHOR

I want to write you a poem
that will tell you just how much
you mean to me.
But the words wouldn't rhyme
and it wouldn't touch you
the way I'd want it to.

I'd like to make you understand
with the sweep of a pen what need is
and that I need you.
But the words would stop
just when you needed them to go on.

I want to sing you a song
that would make you cry inside yourself.
But you wouldn't listen
because the wall you've built around yourself
is so high it's almost impossible to climb.

I'd like to try.

190

YOU ARE SPECIAL

UNKNOWN AUTHOR

"Special" is a word
That is used to describe
Something one-of-a-kind
Like a hug
Or a sunset
Or a person who spreads love
With a smile or kind gesture.
"Special" describes people
Who act from the heart
And keep in mind the hearts of others.
"Special" applies to something
That is admired and precious
And which can never be replaced.
"Special" is the word that best describes you.

191

MOMENTS

UNKNOWN AUTHOR

If there ever were moments more precious,
If there ever were moments more true.
If there ever were moments more wonderful
They're the moments I spend with you.
Though deeply embedded,
You revealed a strength
That was always present within me.
You showed me a love from inside my heart
I never knew I could see
You've strengthened my life with your actions.
By showing you really do care.
Now I know I can turn around
And find that you'll be there.
All the places I've been in search of
Things that never could really be seen.
When all I had to do was look in your eyes
You've shown me what love can mean.

192

FREE SPIRIT

UNKNOWN AUTHOR

I try to capture your spirit with words,
But it is as elusive as the wind.
Ever changing, never twice the same,
Full of boyish mischief one minute,
Then contemplating mysteries beyond
    comprehension,
Yet always beyond the realm of my world.
I stand wordlessly, watching,
As you pass untouchable through my life.

193

WRITING

UNKNOWN AUTHOR

Writing is a special gift.
It's a love for words
That gives you a life.
It brightens your day
If you can express with a pen
All the feelings
You hold within.
Some write poems
With a special flair
That shows their love
And sometimes despair.
Others write books
For which they are known
They become famous
Or they stay unknown.
But it isn't the recognition
That gives them the spirit to write,
It's the feeling from inside —
A kind of insight.
And then there are those

Writing

That have a unique touch.
They write just a little
But they say so much.
Writing is a gift given to few.
Don't ever give it up
Or you won't be you.

194

REMEMBER ME

BY ABIGAIL ADAMS

...Remember me,
As I do you,
With all the tenderness
Which it is possible for one
To feel for another
Which no time can obliterate,
No distance alter,
But which is always the same.

— FROM A LETTER TO JOHN
ADAMS OCTOBER 25, 1782

ORIGINAL POEM ORDER

What follows is the original order of the poems in Laurie's original two books of poetry followed by some loose poems found elsewhere.

© = Denotes a poem from Laurie's original notebooks not included in this book due to copyright.

‡ = Denotes a poem the editor chose not to include for other reasons.

Original Poem Order

Book 1

1. © A Poem for You (by Orson Welles)
2. Love (7) (by Unknown Author)
3. Hold on to Your Dreams (by Unknown Author)
4. The Mystery of Love (by Unknown Author)
5. Far Away Thoughts (by Unknown Author)
6. Poetry (Possibly by Laurie Weissgarber)
7. Beautiful Things (by Unknown Author)
8. Summer Dreams (2) (by Unknown Author)
9. Ocean Romance (by Unknown Author)
10. Summer's End (by Unknown Author)
11. Not to Touch (by Unknown Author)
12. Reflections (1) (by Laurie Weissgarber)
13. The Sea (3) (by Unknown Author)
14. Love Is... (Possibly by Laurie Weissgarber)
15. Graduation (by Unknown Author)
16. Age (Possibly by Laurie Weissgarber)
17. © A Summer Morning (Possibly by Rachel Field)
18. © The Path on the Sea (by Inna Miller)
19. Your Picture (Possibly by Laurie Weissgarber)
20. Gratitude (Possibly by Laurie Weissgarber)
21. © Symptoms of Love (by Robert Graves)
22. Meeting at Night (by Robert Browning)
23. Friendship (3) (by Unknown Author)
24. I'd like to be a Bird (by Unknown Author)
25. © Sunrise (by Audra Weise)
26. Memories (1) (Possibly by Laurie Weissgarber)
27. Once in a Lifetime
28. ‡ The Dream (by Unknown Author)
29. © Because of Love (Menudo)
30. © Inspiration (by Andrew Loyd Webber and Tim Rice, Prologue to Joseph and the Amazing Technicolor Dreamcoat soundtrack)
31. Take A Chance (by Unknown Author)
32. Solitude (by Unknown Author)

Original Poem Order

33. Sometimes (Possibly by Laurie Weissgarber)
34. Seaside Moments (by Unknown Author)
35. Sunset (by Unknown Author)
36. Winter (by Unknown Author)
37. Time (by Unknown Author)
38. Living Treasures (by Unknown Author)
39. Sanctuary (by Unknown Author)
40. Celebration (by Unknown Author)
41. Images (by Unknown Author)
42. Enchantment (by Unknown Author)
43. Harmony (by Unknown Author)
44. Grace (by Unknown Author)
45. Anticipation (by Unknown Author)
46. Miracles (by Unknown Author)
47. © Becoming (by Debra Manning)
48. Simplicity (by Unknown Author)
49. A Wish Come True (by Unknown Author)
50. Colorful Good-Byes (by Unknown Author)
51. Future (by Unknown Author)
52. Imagination (by Unknown Author)
53. Love (5) (by Unknown Author)
54. Love (6) (by Unknown Author)
55. True Love (by Unknown Author)
56. Friendship (2) (by Ludwig Van Beethoven)
57. © My Friend (1) (by Laura Lee Leyman)
58. © Everyone Needs... (by Barbara Gladys)
59. I Ask Myself
60. Let Me Be Your Friend (by Unknown My Friend (2) (by Roger C. Vanhorn)
61. © Good Friends (by Paul Gauguin)
62. Remember Me (by Abigail Adams)
63. © I Thank You (by Franz Liszt)
64. © Distance (by Gordon D. Thompson)
65. Before The Downpour (by Unknown Author)
66. Things Untold, Still Known (by Unknown Author)
67. Love (3) (by Unknown Author)

Original Poem Order

68. For You (by Unknown Author)
69. Writing (by Unknown Author)
70. Moments (by Unknown Author)
71. Letting Go (Possibly by Laurie Weissgarber)
72. The Ocean (2) (by Unknown Author)
73. Memories (2) (by Unknown Author)
74. Free Spirit (by Unknown Author)
75. Let Love Grow (by Unknown Author)
76. Sometime… (Possibly by Laurie Weissgarber)
77. The Ocean (1) (by Unknown Author)
78. Finding Nature (by Unknown Author)
79. Shining (by Unknown Author)
80. I Want (by Unknown Author)
81. Golden (by Unknown Author)
82. Sayings (by Unknown Author)
83. Reflections (2) (Possibly by Laurie Weissgarber)
84. Untitled (Likely By Laurie Weissgarber)
85. Make It Up (by Unknown Author)
86. The Perfect Love (by Unknown Author)
87. Friendship Poem (by Unknown Author)
88. Together (by Unknown Author)
89. Thinking of You (2) (by Unknown Author)
90. Special Feelings (Possibly by Laurie Weissgarber)
91. What Are These Feelings? (by Unknown Author)
92. You Have Such A Positive Outlook on Life (Possibly by Laurie Weissgarber)
93. It Takes More Than Words (by Unknown Author)
94. I need to know (Possibly by Laurie Weissgarber)
95. Silence (Possibly by Laurie Weissgarber)
96. Love Games (Possibly by Laurie Weissgarber)
97. Spring Breezes (Possibly by Laurie Weissgarber)
98. Changing (Possibly by Laurie Weissgarber)
99. Never Blind (Possibly by Laurie Weissgarber)
100. ‡ A Spring Day
101. © Don't Ever…. (by Laine Parsons)
102. A Special Friendship (by Laurie Weissgarber)

Original Poem Order

103. ‡ Our Parting Was Meant To Be
104. © Reflections (by S. McElmon)
105. Faded (Possibly by Laurie Weissgarber)
106. Love (2) (by Unknown Author)
107. A Friend Is Amie (by Unknown Author)
108. The Strongest Kind of Love (by Unknown Author)
109. The Riddle (by Unknown Author)
110. © Life (by Dwayne Williams)
111. A Smile (Possibly by Laurie Weissgarber)
112. Next Time (Possibly by Laurie Weissgarber)
113. Escape (Possibly by Laurie Weissgarber)
114. Eye Contact (by Unknown Author)
115. ‡ The Letter
116. ‡ Passing Thoughts
117. Outburst (Possibly by Laurie Weissgarber)
118. You're Special (by Laurie Weissgarber)
119. You're Mysterious (by Laurie Weissgarber)
120. Too Good to be True (by Laurie Weissgarber)
121. Songs Remind Me Of You (by Laurie Weissgarber)
122. I Can't Fight This Feeling (by Laurie Weissgarber)
123. You're one of my favorite people (Possibly by Laurie Weissgarber)
124. Friends are keepsakes (Possibly by Laurie Weissgarber)
125. You only have to say "Hello" (Possibly by Laurie Weissgarber)
126. The Joy of Your Friendship (by Unknown Author)
127. Three Wishes (Possibly by Laurie Weissgarber)
128. The Most Precious Gift (by Unknown Author)
129. Gathering Memories (Possibly by Laurie Weissgarber)
130. All That's Wished for You (Possibly by Laurie Weissgarber)
131. Friends Are Rare (by Unknown Author)
132. ‡ A Tribute to your Friendship
133. Thinking of You (3) (Possibly by Laurie Weissgarber)

Original Poem Order

Book 2

1. I haven't seen you in awhile (by Susan Polis Schutz)
2. The Magic of a Friend (by Unknown Author)
3. Tranquility (by Unknown Author)
4. The Ocean (3) (Possibly by Laurie Weissgarber)
5. Come Back (Possibly by Laurie Weissgarber)
6. I am Autumn (by Unknown Author)
7. ‡ I'll Know
8. To Have a Dream (by Unknown Author)
9. ‡ For Now
10. Through An Artist's Eyes (by Unknown Author)
11. Having to Write (Possibly by Laurie Weissgarber)
12. Free Flight (Possibly by Laurie Weissgarber)
13. Love (1) (Possibly by Laurie Weissgarber)
14. We Made Each Other Strong (by Unknown Author)
15. Friend (Possibly by Laurie Weissgarber)
16. Take Time (by Ami Lawhorn)
17. ‡ How Much
18. Friendship (4) (by Unknown Author)
19. Small Wonder (Possibly by Laurie Weissgarber)
20. Holding On, Letting Go (by Unknown Author)
21. A True Friend (Possibly by Laurie Weissgarber)
22. Don't Rush In (Possibly by Laurie Weissgarber)
23. Life (1) (by Unknown Author) (Life can travel in circles)
24. All You Can Be (by Unknown Author)
25. Valentine's Day (Possibly by Laurie Weissgarber)
26. Dizzy In Love (Possibly by Laurie Weissgarber)
27. Your Love (Possibly by Laurie Weissgarber)
28. Tears (Possibly by Laurie Weissgarber)
29. Love (4) (Possibly by Laurie Weissgarber)
30. I'm Looking Around (Possibly by Laurie Weissgarber)
31. You (by Unknown Author)
32. Hidden Love (by Unknown Author)
33. Summer Visions (Possibly by Laurie Weissgarber)
34. Sea Shell (Possibly by Laurie Weissgarber)

Original Poem Order

35. Talking On The Phone (Possibly by Laurie Weissgarber)
36. Trusting (Possibly by Laurie Weissgarber)
37. Courage (Possibly by Laurie Weissgarber)
38. Shooting Stars (Possibly by Laurie Weissgarber)
39. Since the Sunrise (Possibly by Laurie Weissgarber)
40. Saturday Night (Possibly by Laurie Weissgarber)
41. Mr. True Love (Possibly by Laurie Weissgarber)
42. The Sea (2) (Possibly by Laurie Weissgarber)
43. Reality (by Carrie J. Myers)
44. Fond Memories (Possibly by Laurie Weissgarber)
45. Spring Is Near (by Carrie J. Myers)
46. Modern World (Possibly by Laurie Weissgarber)
47. Living in the Past (by Unknown Author)
48. You Are Special (by Unknown Author)
49. My Best Friend (Possibly by Laurie Weissgarber)
50. Untitled (Likely by Laurie Weissgarber)
51. Why Good Looks (by Laurie Weissgarber)
52. Life (3) (by Unknown Author) (Time Life's most precious gift.)
53. Artist Anonymous (Possibly by Laurie Weissgarber)
54. An Aunt, A Friend (by Unknown Author)
55. The Old Oak Tree (Possibly by Laurie Weissgarber)
56. Mysterious Surfer (Possibly by Laurie Weissgarber)
57. Summer Dreams (1) (Possibly by Laurie Weissgarber)
58. Parent's Advice (Possibly by Laurie Weissgarber)
59. The Beach (Possibly by Laurie Weissgarber)
60. Only Time Will Tell (Possibly by Laurie Weissgarber)
61. In Touch (Possibly by Laurie Weissgarber)
62. Broken Friends (Possibly by Laurie Weissgarber)
63. A Beginning (Possibly by Laurie Weissgarber)
64. Dreams (by Unknown Author)
65. Clouds (Possibly by Laurie Weissgarber)
66. A Fantasy (Possibly by Laurie Weissgarber)
67. The Sands of Time
68. Good Ol' Snoopy (Possibly by Laurie Weissgarber)
69. The Little Mermaid (Possibly by Laurie Weissgarber)

Original Poem Order

70. Forget Me Not (by Unknown Author)
71. Weatherly Emotions (Possibly by Laurie Weissgarber)
72. A Thought Apart (Possibly by Laurie Weissgarber)
73. Thinking of You (1) (Possibly by Laurie Weissgarber)
74. What Music Can Do (Possibly by Laurie Weissgarber)
75. Dream Your Life Away (Possibly by Laurie Weissgarber)
76. My Loved One (Possibly by Laurie Weissgarber)
77. Cinquain (Possibly by Laurie Weissgarber)
78. Stage (Possibly by Laurie Weissgarber)
79. What Is Happiness (by Star Myers)
80. The Stars (Possibly by Laurie Weissgarber)
81. The Sea of Life (Possibly by Laurie Weissgarber)
82. © A Teardrop (by Tina Thompson)
83. An Ocean of Feelings (Possibly by Laurie Weissgarber)
84. The Kite (Possibly by Laurie Weissgarber)

Loose Poems

1. The Sea (1) (by Laurie Weissgarber)
2. Teenagers (by Unknown Author)
3. Wonder Is... (by Laurie Weissgarber)
4. Friendship (1) (Possibly by Laurie Weissgarber)

PHOTOS OF LAURIE

The following photos show Laurie chronologically throughout her life.

Photos of Laurie

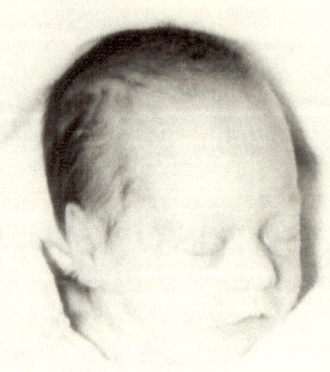

3 Weeks

Photos of Laurie

Nov 1967 - Laurie with toy Monkey Zippy

Photos of Laurie

1972 - School Yearbook

Photos of Laurie

December 1975 - Playing Clue

Photos of Laurie

January 1977 - Behind firehouse in Katonah, NY

Photos of Laurie

1982 - Senior Year of High School

Photos of Laurie

1986 - Dutchess Community College Graduation in NY

Photos of Laurie

1988 - First Wedding

Photos of Laurie

November 1997 - Disneyworld Themepark

Photos of Laurie

2003

Photos of Laurie

2006

Photos of Laurie

2014

Photos of Laurie

June 2018 - Yosemite National Park

Photos of Laurie

Laurie with Family

June 13th, 2015 - Wedding, Top: Steve Harden (Husand), Ryan Vogel (Son), Leo Vogel (Son). Bottom: Laurie Jean Weissgarber, John Weissgarber (Father).

THANKS

The editor thanks the following people, in alphabetical order, for their support in writing and researching this book.

- Brenda Martin: Laurie's friend
- Cherrie Reinhardt: Laurie's sister
- Jane Gregory: Laurie's High School English teacher
- Kim Woodstead: Laurie's cousin, whom she exchanged many of these poems with during high school
- Mary Hulsizer: Laurie's friend
- Steve Harden: Laurie's husband
- The Dutchess Community College's Archives Library staff

ABOUT THE EDITOR

A person never gets used to the fact that their loved one is never coming back.

— LAURIE JEAN WEISSGARBER, SEPT 27TH, 1984

Leo Vogel is the proud editor of this poetry collection by his late mother, Laurie Jean Weissgarber, who he misses every day. Leo grew up in the Mid-Hudson Valley and now lives around the world, as a digital nomad, working remotely as he travels to explore new countries to immerse himself in other cultures as a means of learning more about himself and the world in which he lives.

He enjoys hiking through national parks, attending international concerts, and cherishing the moments spent with his friends around the globe. He also makes it a priority to read books that expand his mind. Through the publication of this collection, Leo aspires to honor his mother's memory and ensure that her words and favorite poems touch the hearts of others, providing solace, inspiration, and a lasting legacy.

You can learn more about Leo at his website LeoVogel.com

ABOUT THE AUTHOR

Laurie Jean Weissgarber was a loving mother and creative woman whose warmth and kindness brightened the lives of her friends, family, and colleagues. Born on Nov. 13th, 1963 at 7:42 AM, 3 pounds 12.5 ounces, at Northern Westchester Hospital in Mount Kisco, New York she was raised by her parents John Weissgarber and Bertha Woodstead. Laurie graduated from Arlington High School (1983) and Dutchess Community College (1986) before starting a career in childcare services.

In 1985, at the age of 22, while still in college, she started compiling a collection of poems into two notebooks including poems by her and those she cherished. This collection had been started during high school; when she had exchanged poems with her cousin Kim Woodstead.

Laurie chose to pursue a life focused on caring for children—not only her own but also through her career and volunteering. She married in 1988, becoming Laurie Jean Vogel, and had two sons: Ryan Vogel and Leo Vogel. In 2015, she married her second husband, Steve Harden, and became Laurie Jean Harden.

In late 2019, Laurie began to develop early-onset frontal lobe aphasia, and her condition rapidly worsened. It was during the final stages of her illness that her older son discovered her collection of poems among her arts & crafts supplies. On May 15, 2023, Laurie died peacefully in her sleep in Rhinebeck, New York.

Throughout her life one of Laurie's biggest joys was hot air balloons. She loved going to local balloon festivals and enjoyed balloon chases. On September 1st, 2023 she took her last balloon ride when her husband sprinkled some of her ashes over the Mid-Hudson Valley.

For updates and more information visit LaurieJean.com

www.ingramcontent.com/pod-product-compliance
Lightning Source LLC
Chambersburg PA
CBHW030447100526
44580CB00001B/14